# THE COMEDIAN WHO CHOKED TO DEATH ON A PIE...

## AND THE MAN WHO QUIT SMOKING AT 116

*A Collection of Incredible Lives and Unbelievable Deaths*

# THE COMEDIAN WHO CHOKED TO DEATH ON A PIE...

## AND THE MAN WHO QUIT SMOKING AT 116

*A Collection of Incredible Lives
and Unbelievable Deaths*

BY THE EDITORS OF *FORTEAN TIMES*

CADER BOOKS • NEW YORK

Andrews and McMeel
A Universal Press Syndicate Company
Kansas City

*Thank you for buying this Cader Book*—we hope you enjoy it. And thanks as well to the store that sold you this, and the hardworking sales rep who sold it to them. It takes a lot of people to make a book (even a skinny one). Here are some of the many who were instrumental:

EDITORIAL:
Rufus Griscom,
Jake Morrissey, Dorothy O'Brien, Regan Brown
DESIGN:
Charles Kreloff and Orit Mardkha-Tenzer
COPY EDITING/PROOFING:
Nanette Maxim, Linda Olle, Brian Bendlin
PRODUCTION:
Carol Coe, Cathy Kirkland
LEGAL:
Renee Schwartz, Esq.
FORTEAN CONSULTANTS:
Mike Dash, Paul Sieveking, John Innes
COVER PHOTOS:
Archive Photos/American Stock

IF YOU WOULD LIKE to share any thoughts about this book, or are interested in other books by us, please write to:

CADER BOOKS
38 E. 29 Street
New York, NY, 10016
Or visit our cool new web site: http://www.caderbooks.com

Library of Congress Cataloging-in-Publication Data

The comedian who choked to death on a pie — and the man who quit smoking at 116 :
a collection of incredible lives and unbelievable deaths /
by the editors of Fortean Times. —1st ed.
p.    cm.
"Cader books."
Includes bibliographical references.
ISBN: 0-8362-2147-8
1. Biography—20th century—Anecdotes.  2. Death—Anecdotes.
3. Curiosities and wonders.  I. Fortean times.
CT120C646     1996
920—dc20
[B]      96-38625      CIP

November 1996

First edition
10 9 8 7 6 5 4 3 2 1

# CONTENTS

———•◆•———

# INTRODUCTION

———•◆•———

Peple do the funniest things, in life and in death. The editors of *Fortean Times* magazine have collected some of the most memorable here—true tales of hilarious deaths and wise words from some of the oldest people in the world about how to live and how not to.

History is littered with famous and curious casualties. The Greek playwright Aeschylus supposedly died when an eagle mistook his bald head for a rock and dropped a tortoise on it, hoping to break its shell. Attila the Hun conquered half of Europe but died of a nosebleed on his wedding night. Writer Arnold Bennett drank a glass of water in Paris to prove it was safe and promptly died of typhoid. Yet famous deaths are already well cataloged, so we have opted instead for marking the deaths of the less well-known.

Over the past twenty-odd years, the Strange Deaths section of *Fortean Times*—a British monthly magazine of news and research on all things weird—has chronicled many of the peculiar circumstances under which we depart on our last journey. This collection gathers a number of classic tales from the column and includes many more besides, exhumed from the bulging folders of the *Fortean Times* archives.

Although everyone's time must come, some of us persist longer than others. We cap off this collection of the Grim Reaper's greatest hits with testimonials from some of his greatest misses: accounts of the oldest people in the world, gathered in the "Still Ticking" chapter at the end of this volume.

It seems as though the best way to survive longer than 100 years is to live in a mountainous region away from the stresses of industrial life and high-calorie diets. One such area is the highlands of Guangxi province in China, where the locals drink "longevity wine" made from lizards, snakes, dog and deer penises and about 40 herbs and grasses. Alternately, we can listen to advice from the old-timers themselves. Manoel de Moura, a Brazilian who claimed to be over 160, proclaimed: "I don't own anything and I don't worry about anything," while Prom Kaewerorarm, 115, suggested we eat "five hot, fried chili peppers every day to keep you regular." On the other hand Jackson Pollard, allegedly 123 in 1990, advised, "avoid alcohol, eat good vegetables, and never, never get married to no skinny woman."

Is every story in these pages nothing but the truth? We cannot know for sure. Though the stories herein are all faithful to newspaper accounts, newspapers these days have been known to embroider stories or print contemporary legend as fact. We could not check every case, but we present all of our references at the end of the book.

A debt of gratitude is due to the many readers of *Fortean Times* who have sent news clippings over the years, without whom neither the magazine nor this book would exist. There are far too many to mention by name, but this book is dedicated to each and every one. We wish them a full life and hope they clip to a ripe old age!

—STEVE MOORE AND PAUL SIEVEKING

# THE COMEDIAN WHO CHOKED TO DEATH ON A PIE...

## AND THE MAN WHO QUIT SMOKING AT 116

*A Collection of Incredible Lives and Unbelievable Deaths*

# CUPID'S DEADLY DARTS

———◆———

*We begin where life begins: with love, or at least with sex. On occasion, though, that's where it all ends, too. The best way to go, or the worst? We can't ask the dead. Take these stories as you will—the romance of death, or the death of romance.*

———◆———

JIMMY "THE BEARD" FERROZZO, the 40-year-old assistant manager of the Condor Club, a topless bar in the North Beach section of San Francisco, was found crushed to death between a trick piano and the club's 12-foot-high ceiling. Beneath him, naked and hysterical, was exotic dancer Teresa Hill, 23. The gutted Steinway baby grand that sandwiched them was routinely used by the club's star dancer to descend from her dressing room onto the stage. Apparently, after closing time the night before, the couple had decided to make love on the piano, and in the process they somehow tripped the power switch that raised it to the ceiling. Ferrozzo died of asphyxiation due to crushing; his companion was only saved by the cushioning effect of his body.

◆

A SIMILAR CALAMITY occurred in West Akron, Ohio, to Daisy Gladden, 20, and her lover James Daniels, Jr., 26. On January 17, 1988, after indulging in drugs and alcohol, they decided to make love in the front seat of a car parked inside an abandoned garage. It was all too much for 168-pound Daniels, who died in the act and trapped Daisy beneath him. With only a thin raincoat to cover her, and suffering from hypothermia, she was discovered four days later when a tow-truck driver outside the garage heard her screams. She was still wedged beneath the decomposing body of her naked lover.

Sachi Hidaka and his wife, Tomio, of Chiba, Japan, were overwhelmed in the act. The shy couple, both 34 years old, had waited 14 years before making love for the first time, in 1992. It proved too much, and both died of heart attacks, although neither had a history of heart trouble.

AT A WEDDING RECEPTION in Beijing, China, in 1987, the groom, Min Chou Lin, reportedly kissed the bride to death. They were both found unconscious on a sofa, locked in each others' arms, and were rushed to the hospital. The bride died, of heart palpitations brought on by the excitement.

• ◆ •

IN 1990, JOE BRAYBOY'S WIFE, PATRICIA, suspected that he was visiting a lover, so she set off with a friend to find him. Driving down a street in Houston, Texas, she spotted what she thought was Joe's gray Volvo parked beside a strange house. She pounded on the door and began to force her way inside. Hearing the commotion, a neighbor grabbed his shotgun and shot Patricia dead. As her friend fled screaming down the road, she noticed the correct gray Volvo parked in a different driveway, a few houses away.

• ◆ •

A TEENAGE BOY NAMED Jochen grew up with three girls— Dunja, Petra and Christina—in a special home for deaf-mutes in Heilbronn, Germany. In 1980, Dunja fell in love with Jochen. One day they walked to an old deserted bomb shelter, where they made love for the first time, and Dunja cried with happiness. While she lay with her eyes closed, Jochen killed her, hitting her on the head with a bottle and stabbing her several times with a pair of scissors. Why? It appears that the romance hadn't gone over well with the other two girls who, using sign language, threatened suicide if the affair continued, yet offered love if it didn't. All three conspirators were found guilty of murder, but were given only two-year suspended sentences.

Marian Paler, 36, in Resita, Romania, caught her trapeze-artist husband in a compromising position with another woman. A few hours later, Marian guffawed loudly during a critical moment in their performance when her husband required total concentration. He fell to his death from the flying trapeze.

THREE-FOOT, NINE-INCH Martha Farrand, professionally known as the Vest-Pocket Venus, was loved by her two high-wire partners in a Hungarian circus act. Jealousy overcame caution and a fight broke out one night high above the audience, causing both men to plunge to their deaths in the ring.

Perhaps the strangest of Eastern European circus love triangles was the 1993 incident that involved a married couple and a horse. Trainer Hanibal Cantori went to the stable to give his stallion, Galbenus, some sugar, and discovered his wife, Laura, having intercourse with the animal. When she confessed to regularly seeking satisfaction with Galbenus, Hanibal strangled her with a silk scarf and then committed suicide.

•◆•

Beauty queen Helene Momescu, of Cetatea, Romania, juggled five lovers at the same time. When they eventually learned about one another, they decided on a drastic course of action. The five met at a deserted house one night in 1978, each armed with a revolver, a bottle of liquor, a candle, and a signed letter explaining his intentions. Drinking steadily, they lit the candles, having agreed that once the candles burned out, they would begin shooting and the survivor would claim the girl. The last candle sputtered, the shots duly rang out, and in the morning all five men were found dead. Helene was run out of town and forbidden to return.

•◆•

Sophia Kneen, a 30-year-old oil broker, was hugged to death by her spurned lover. She and commodities dealer Tim Brockman, 32, had shared an apartment in Fulham, England. Kneen wanted to end their eight-year relationship after a series of tempestuous rows. In October 1992, after drinking with a friend and joking that his plans for the evening were "murder, then suicide," Brockman returned to the apartment. In what investigators suggested may have begun as a show of affection, Brockman squeezed the life out of Sophia; bruising to her shoulders and back suggested that she had died of "crush" asphyxiation, a method of murder popularized by the 19th-century Scottish body snatchers Burke and Hare, models for *Dr. Jekyll and Mr. Hyde*. Brockman laid her on the bed, wreathed her head with flowers, and some hours later, slashed his throat, chest and wrists before hanging himself from a ceiling beam nearby.

Government officials in Istanbul, Turkey, were forced to issue a health warning in 1990 about people making love on roofs during sultry summer evenings. At least a dozen people were said to die each year when, after a night on the roof tiles, they fell asleep and rolled off the edge.

In 1993, William Nelson of Santa Ana, California, died in bed after an argument about money with his Egyptian-born wife, Omaima. A rape crisis counselor by day and a hooker by night, 24-year-old Omaima hit her 54-year-old husband with a lamp, then tied him to a mattress before dressing up in red shoes, a red hat and blood-red lipstick. She then hacked the 224-pound man to pieces and skinned him, barbecued his ribs and ate them, and finally ground up the rest of the body in the garbage-disposal unit in her kitchen. Sent to jail for 27 years, she told the judge she was "a warm person who wouldn't harm a mosquito."

•◆•

Patricia Orionno of France got fed up with her husband, Jean-Louis, demanding too much sex. In 1988, she tried to overdose him with sleeping tablets, but he merely fell asleep. She slashed his wrists and gassed him—that didn't work either. Then she tried smothering him, but he woke up. On the fifth attempt, she stabbed him eight times, and at last he died. French courts make allowances for crimes of passion, however, and she was freed.

ALSO BROUGHT TO DISASTER by his sexual appetite was jazz trumpeter Joe "Pootie" Newman, who had played with the Count Basie and Lionel Hampton bands. Described as having "a masterly control of his instrument, a uniquely rhythmic way with the valves," he was also known to be a ladies' man. In 1989, Newman submitted his instrument to the surgeon's knife for an inflatable penile implant, but the operation failed. A build-up of pressure brought about a series of embarrassing explosions, including one in a restaurant, that resulted in internal bleeding. In July 1992 he died of a blood clot in the brain. Newman's last album was called *Hangin' Out*.

• ◆ •

HIGH ABOVE A PRIVATE BEACH in Naples in 1984, 48-year-old Salvatore Ancoretti sat on a rock, ogling the nude sunbathers who lay beneath him. Alas, the rock gave way and Ancoretti plunged 100 feet to the beach below, dying on impact, with his binoculars still clutched in his hands.

# WEDDING WOES

---

*Romance is followed by marriage—or at least that used to be the idea. Though weddings are often counted among life's high points, misfortune occasionally reduces them to low points.*

---

NO ONE TOLD GERMAN-BORN bride Amy Weltz that it's an old tradition in Australia for newlyweds to smear wedding cake on each other's faces. When new husband Chas pushed a slice into her face at their September 1993 reception in Brisbane, she hit him over the head with a wine bottle. He died instantly.

---

WEARING AN ARTIFICIAL BUN to enhance her natural hair, bride Thankamma Mathai, 20, looked radiantly happy as she entered the church at Trivandrum, India, in July 1977. Watched by the priest, groom, relatives and friends, she walked down the aisle, then suddenly collapsed. As the guests rushed to her side, Mathai gave a groan and died on the church floor. A doctor found the mark of a snake's bite on the nape of her neck. Mathai had worn the hairpiece during a dress rehearsal at home the previous night, and had then placed it in a corner of the room. A small, poisonous snake had apparently coiled itself up inside the bun overnight and bitten her while she was on her way to the church, yet no sign of the snake was found.

• ◆ •

IN JUNE 1993, despite having been hospitalized by a heart attack the day before, angina sufferer Irene Guy was determined to go through with her wedding to Brian Holmes on her 48th birthday. She discharged herself from the hospital in Otley, West Yorkshire, England, and proceeded with the ceremony, though four hours later than originally planned. Two hours after the service, she collapsed at the reception and died before reaching the hospital. Doctors said she would probably have died anyway, even if she had stayed in the hospital, so perhaps it was worth it after all.

> Immediately after he was married at Council Bluffs, Iowa, in June 1979, Greg Cundiff, age 23, was stricken by nerves and heat. He fainted, hit his head on the altar steps and never regained consciousness.

WEDDINGS AND MONEY seem to be a dangerous combination. A couple from Shanxi province in northern China gave the equivalent of $3 as a June 1991 wedding gift to their nephew, while other relatives gave $7.20. The sums are small, but China is poor; the difference is what counts. Unable to bear the other relatives' scorn at their paltry gift, and worried about future wedding gifts for other nephews and nieces, Yang Baosheng hanged himself after his wife, Qu Junmei, drowned herself.

IN JUNE 1987, a newlywed couple in North Carolina was given a hot-air balloon ride as a wedding gift. The balloon became entangled in power lines, and while the wife was unhurt, the pilot suffered electrical burns and the groom was killed.

When two brothers in Ramtha, Jordan, got married in a double ceremony, a joint reception was held in September 1990. As the brides were dancing and singing with a group of women guests, the dance floor collapsed beneath them. Appallingly, there was a cesspool under the floor, and they all plunged into it. Thirteen were killed, including both brides, and ten women from the same family were among the dead. Both bridegrooms were in another room at the time and escaped the tragedy.

THEY WERE STILL PARTYING 11 HOURS after the wedding of Max Hoffmann, in Traunreut, Bavaria, in October 1991. Unfortunately, Hoffmann, 39, went berserk when his camera failed to work, and gave his father a black eye. His mother, Astrid, then stabbed her son to death with a kitchen knife in front of the bride and 40 wedding guests.

• ◆ •

SOME WEDDING CEREMONIES are more ghoulish than others. Zhang Jiahua, 44, was arrested in Shanxi province in February 1992 when railway officials searched his baggage. Inside, they found the body of a woman who had died two years earlier. Zhang had dug her up in the southern province of Sichuan and transported her across China for eight days, so that she could be "married" to a man who had died a bachelor. According to Chinese tradition, dying when unmarried is unlucky, and posthumous marriages have more than once been arranged. Zhang had been paid the equivalent of $60 to act as "matchmaker for the dead."

Rissa Nasrul died just before her wedding in Kabul, Afghanistan. The wedding ceremony, in September 1990, was to be her eighth. She was 101 years old, and her 48-year-old prospective bridegroom said: "I guess the prospect was far too exciting for her."

# TEMPER TEMPER

———◆———

*The daily frustrations of life are merely annoying to some and absolutely unbearable to others. When people reach their breaking point, anything can happen.*

———◆———

THOMAS CORLETT, 58, a senior executive officer at the German Department of Employment, had strict ideas about where the mustard should be placed on the dining table. His Austrian wife of 15 years, Erika, 63, had her own opinions. In December 1985, an argument broke out. "It was her fault," he said. "I always placed my newspaper on one side of my plate, the mustard on the other. But she moved my paper and put the mustard in its place instead, saying, 'That's where I want it, and that's where I will put it.' She started shouting and kept on and on about the paper. She raised her hand and I thought she was going to hit me. I just grabbed her by the throat and we fell to the floor." After that, he strangled her.

◆

FORTY-EIGHT-YEAR-OLD Michael S. Allen of Markham, Illinois, was sick to death of his 88-year-old mother's habit of watching *The Cosby Show*. Allen couldn't stand the series and finally, in July 1986, he shot his mother several times with a .22-caliber rifle and left her to die on the living-room floor while he turned himself in to the police.

Psychiatrist Oscar Dominguez, 45, shot a woman patient in his São Paulo, Brazil, office, as she told him about her sex life. At his trial he explained: "I couldn't take those nutcases anymore…"

FOR MARLENE LOVE, 39, of Calgary, Alberta, Canada, the breaking point came in October 1991 when her 38-year-old husband, Douglas, settled down to watch his fifth football game of the day on satellite TV. She shot him in the back of the head with a rifle. Love told police: "There was no food in the house and I kept asking him to give me some money and the car keys so I could go to the store, but he kept saying, 'Shut up! Can't you see I'm watching a game?' "

• ◆ •

GIOVANNI MANCUSO of Messina, Italy, was an amateur pianist who practiced daily on his grand piano. The main drawback was that his repertoire consisted of only one piece, and his annoyed neighbor Pietro Pettinato eventually shot him for it. The tune Mancuso played repeatedly? Chopin's "Funeral March."

• ◆ •

SOMETIMES THE NOISE that drives people past the point of sanity is a natural one. Near Perth, Australia, in March 1991, a 22-year-old drug addict named Joseph Taylor got fed up with the coughing of his brother Dale, 16. He was so fed up, in fact, that he locked him in the trunk of his car, doused the auto with gasoline, set it on fire and burned Dale to death. "I could hear my brother yelling and screaming, but he'd just coughed one time too many," Taylor told police.

IN CESENA, ITALY, a 10-year-old student named Andrea Casanova routinely went home with his friend Roberto Pulzelli to help Pulzelli with his math homework. Roberto's 18-year-old sister, Pasqua, felt her little brother was relying too much on outside assistance, so after several scoldings she decided to put an end to it by taking her father's shotgun and blasting Andrea to death.

Walter Jeurgens, a German 19-year-old, was served eggs at every meal by his new wife, Elfreide, 18. He got so fed up with it that he left home, but when he decided to return, in September 1990, Elfreide fried up some eggs for him. He shot her dead, and remarked after his arrest: "I used to like eggs."

A SCIENCE TEACHER in St. Marcel, Normandy, accused a 15-year-old boy of stealing a lightbulb in March 1978. The teacher kept the boy in after-school detention, and the next morning told the entire class about the incident. As the teacher did so, the humiliated boy stood up, pulled out a revolver and shot him dead. The boy then went into another classroom and put a bullet through his own head.

•◆•

JANET SMITH, 28, walked into a grocery store in Gresham, Oregon, on August 21, 1994, and sat down in an aisle, all the while holding a knife to the throat of her Siamese cat. Told by police to drop the knife, she threatened to kill the cat. Suddenly, she jumped up and began walking toward the police, who sprayed her with pepper Mace. She then raised the knife above her head and charged at the police, who shot her dead. The cat escaped and could not be found.

At Tokyo's Takushoku University, students at a karate club kicked 19-year-old Tetsuya Mori to death and severely injured another student in July 1986. The ill-fated two had failed to wash their uniforms.

SIXTY-FIVE-YEAR-OLD Salvatore Romano from Agrigento, Italy, decided that his daughter's fiancé was too ugly for her. So when 30-year-old Calogero Lumia turned up at Romano's house in March 1993, Romano opened the door and shot Lumia with a pistol. He explained to police: "If he'd married my Anna, I'd have had to look at him for the rest of my life."

•◆•

IN FEBRUARY 1993, 47-year-old shopkeeper Luigi D'Alessio shot his doctor dead in Foggia, Italy, when the doctor said he couldn't cure D'Alessio's cold.

In St. Louis in December 1986, Nathan Hicks, 35, became enraged when his younger brother, Herbert, 33, used six rolls of toilet paper in two days. There were still two rolls left, but Nathan shot Herbert in the chest with a .22 rifle, killing him.

KNIFE IN HAND, Chen Bohong of Liuzhou, China, was slaughtering his pig in October 1987 when tax man Sun Taichang turned up and presented Chen with a $1.50 pig-tax bill. Outraged, Chen slaughtered the tax collector and was duly executed for his crime.

•◆•

ROYAL NAVY ENGINEER Derek Guy had a trivial argument with his wife, Sharon, over a slice of toast and marmalade at their home in Market Harborough, England, in July 1988. He thereupon ran into the road, lay down and waited for a car to run over him. A few minutes later, a Ford Escort did just that, running over his head and killing him.

•◆•

EDWARD MUSGROVE, 32, attacked his estranged wife as she began her evening route as a Los Angeles bus driver. He grabbed the steering wheel, causing the bus to veer off the road, hit a tree and crash into a brick wall. The wife was not injured, but Musgrove was hurled through the windshield into the wall and decapitated.

# LOONY LOSSES

*Though we commonly refer to the Reaper as grim, some demises are so ludicrous we begin to suspect the old boy of having a sense of humor. Dark, perhaps, but one can almost hear an eerie chuckle as the following tales unfold.*

TO SUPPORT HER AMPLE frame, Berbel Zumner, 23, wore a bra reinforced with metal wires. These conducted a bolt of lightning that killed her as she was walking through a park in Vienna.

JOBLESS DANIEL PITIORET, 43, decided he wanted to die, and asked his friend Thierry Dierick to help him do the deed. Dierick, 29 and also jobless, wasn't up for it, but Pitioret offered $9,750 and told Dierick he would write a letter to prove he'd asked Dierick to do it. Pitioret threatened to commit suicide anyway if Dierick didn't help. So in March 1993, they went for a last supper at the best restaurant in Bourg-en-Bresse, in southeastern France. Pitioret paid the $300 bill by check and the two vanished into the night. Later, Pitioret's body was found in a wood, his head almost blown off by a shotgun fired from behind. Police found his ID card and a check stub made out to

Dierick, on which was written "payment for a contract to kill me." They immediately arrested Dierick and, despite Pitioret's letter, charged him with murder. Worse still, the check bounced.

Karate brown-belt and Thai boxing enthusiast Scott Kell, 23, lost his balance doing high kicks and plunged to his death through an open window on the tenth floor of a tower block in Salford, England, on July 6, 1994.

MICHAEL TOWNSEND, a fit 60-year-old from Bath, England, was found dead on the beach at Woolacombe, North Devon, in April 1982. He was wearing only his underpants, kneeling, with his head buried in the sand.

• ◆ •

A NAKED MAN RUNNING across New York's Brooklyn Bridge in May 1993, singing "Oh, What a Beautiful Morning!" was run over by a car and killed.

In January 1978, two friends in Thonburi, Thailand, argued over that old chestnut: Which came first, the chicken or the egg? A fight broke out between them, and the man arguing for the chicken accidentally killed the man arguing for the egg.

IN JUNE 1987, the very same chicken-and-egg dispute broke out among a group of men in the Philippines. On the side of the chicken were Georgio Santos and Tomas Ja, a pair of barbers from the town of Tamban; the egg men were José Martas and Francisco Ferre. Thinking he'd won, Ja cried out: "You are fools! What I say proves that the chicken came first!" His subsequent argument is not recorded, but it appears to have upset his opponents. They pulled out pistols and shot both barbers dead.

In what may strike some as an even more pointless argument from June 1987, a 29-year-old man in the Philippines stabbed to death his 35-year-old elder brother and wounded a drinking companion in a dispute over whether Imelda Marcos was prettier than the Princess of Wales. The dead man supported Princess Diana.

UNFORTUNATELY HE WHO laughs longest may laugh for the last time. Alexander Mitchell, 50, a bricklayer from King's Lynn, England, died laughing in March 1975 while watching the TV comedy *The Goodies*. He had recently eaten, and after 25 minutes of laughing on a full stomach, his heart failed while he was watching a fight between a set of bagpipes and a black pudding.

• ◆ •

MRS. DOROTHY JOHNSON, a 72-year-old widow from Birmingham, England, also found something a bit too funny. In October 1992, her two-year-old great-grandson offered her a jelly sweet before taking off his hat to show her his new, extremely short haircut. Mrs. Johnson found this so hilarious that she burst into uncontrollable laughter, and choked to death on the sweet.

•◆•

MORE CURIOUS STILL WAS the case of Charles Lecuere, 55, of Bordeaux, France, who had always had a great fear of rats. He and his wife, Monique, 52, kept their marriage fresh by surprising each other with special outfits. In June 1988, Monique bought a brunette wig and left it on a shelf in the bathroom. Before she could put it on, Charles went to clean his teeth, but was not wearing his glasses. He mistook the wig for a huge rat that he thought had crawled in through the window and was about to attack him. He died of a heart attack.

An unnamed Austin, Texas, man of 35 became entangled in a garden hose and strangled himself while trying to get free. He was found in a field behind an Austin food plant in May 1983, with the hose wrapped around his waist and chest.

SOMETIMES MOTHER NATURE herself is the joker. In February 1982, David M. Grundman of Phoenix, Arizona, went into the desert and fired repeatedly at the trunk of a giant saguaro cactus for target practice. The large pitchfork-shaped cactus is Arizona's state plant and an endangered species. As Grundman fired off his last round, the heavy upper section of the cactus, 23 feet long, toppled over and fell on him, spearing him to death.

IF CACTI ARE VENGEFUL, perhaps palms are simply malevolent. In June 1993, Armando Pinelli, 70, had an argument with another man over who should sit in the only chair in the shade of a palm tree in a park at Foggia, Italy. Pinelli won the argument and contentedly sat back to read his newspaper. The palm tree then fell on him, killing him.

• ◆ •

FALLING, THOUGH FROM a far lesser height, also brought about the end of 73-year-old Robert Hamm of Rochester, New York. He had a standard-size, galvanized metal trash can on his front porch and fell into it in January 1989, rear-end first. He was stuck in the can up to his armpits, with his legs sticking in the air. Three days passed. On the first day, an 11-year-old newspaper-delivery girl waved to him and said hello; he waved back and seemed to mumble something, and she went on her way. On the second day, the postman saw his hand move, but ignored it. On the third day, the newspaper girl's mother went to investigate and found him still there, but by that time he'd died of heart failure.

And still they fall. Gerard Hommel, a veteran of six Mount Everest climbing expeditions, was changing a lightbulb in the kitchen of his home in Nantes, France, in October 1993. He fell off the ladder, cracked his head on the sink, and died.

AN UNNAMED MAN of 56 tricked his way into a house in Alicante, Spain, in May 1991, by claiming to be a sewing-machine repairman. Once inside, he grabbed 18,000 pesetas (about $120) and ran off. As the woman chased him, he tripped, swallowed his false teeth, and choked to death.

IN MARCH 1993, cabbie Alla Dalhanna's habit of chewing his sunglasses was the death of him. His car was rammed by another auto in El-Alamein, Egypt, and his chewing became choking, with fatal results.

Ramon Barrera of Mexico, a man once famous for playing "the world's smallest harmonica," gave an exhibition performance in Iguala in January 1994. In a moment of excitement, he swallowed the harmonica and choked to death.

SOMETIMES WE DON'T KNOW whether to laugh or cry; with this tale, though, we wince. Hosiery knitter Hardial Singh, 41, took a bath at his home in Leicester, England, in November 1992. Afterward, he tried to balance his backside on a broomstick while opening a window. He slipped, impaled himself on the broom handle and fled the bathroom screaming. He was taken to a hospital, where an operation was performed to remove his injured bowel, but he died two weeks later when blood clots reached his lungs.

•◆•

IN JUNE 1984, a Chinese newspaper published a photograph of three smiling soldiers posing on a railway track, their backs to a speeding train that killed them a split second later. The paper, *China Law*, did not explain why the photographer, a fellow soldier who was presumed to have jumped clear in time, failed to warn them of the approaching danger.

•◆•

EAGER TO TRY ON A NEW $1,100 TOUPEE in January 1992, shop manager Claude Jules, 53, of Abbeville, France, stopped his car, dabbed on the special glue and set the wig in place. Then he lit a cigarette. Fumes from the wig glue ignited and the car exploded, killing him instantly.

●◆●

DONALD TOLLETT, 60, died from suffocation on February 11, 1995, after a freak weather phenomenon called a stythe caused a drop in air pressure, sucking carbon dioxide from a vacant coal mine. Tollett was walking through the Karva Woodcrafts factory in Widdrington Station, England, accompanied by eight-year-old David Wind and a collie, when he and the dog were overcome.

# SNOW JOBS

---◆◆◆---

*Even ridiculous ends can be chilling. When the cold hand of death settles on our shoulder, could there be a more appropriate setting than a snowy field or a glacier?*

---◆◆◆---

TONY BOWERS, 7, of Lawley Green, Shropshire, England, was killed by a snowball in January 1980. With the help of his brother and a friend, he had been rolling a giant snowball up a hill near his home, with the intention of letting it roll down. Unfortunately, the five-foot-wide snowball got stuck, so Tony tried to free it by clearing the snow in front of it. He did his work too well, and the snowball rolled over him, pinning him face down in the snow. Although the other boys kicked the snowball to pieces and freed him, he died of crushing and asphyxiation.

◆◆◆

EVEN THOUGH TONY'S death was described as a million-to-one freak accident, exactly the same thing happened to Robin Morrell, 12, of Hereford, England, in April 1989. His snowball was only four feet wide, but it, too, rolled on top of him and pinned him face down. His brother found Robin with only his feet sticking out from the snowball, and he suffocated before he could be freed.

IN FEBRUARY 1991, Piera Rutelli, 40, was driving through a tunnel near Genoa, Italy. A large icicle fell from the tunnel ceiling, penetrated the roof of Rutelli's car, and killed her.

• ◆ •

AN ACCIDENT OF AN even more bizarre type befell Sherry Gados, 34, in December 1988. Having apparently lost her keys, she tried to break into her own Dayton, Ohio, house through the pantry window. Why she didn't rouse her husband, John, who was sleeping inside, is far from clear, as is why she was wearing only underwear and socks. Nonetheless, the window somehow closed on her foot, leaving her dangling upside down outdoors. An element of farce entered the tragedy when she was spotted by next-door neighbor Wilma Johnson, but ignored. For some inexplicable reason, Wilma managed to convince herself that Sherry was nothing but a shop-window dummy hung outside the window, and only investigated some hours later when she saw Sherry still there. By that time, Sherry was covered with snow, and had died of exposure.

• ◆ •

PERHAPS STRANGER STILL was the fate that befell five German glider pilots over the Rhine Valley in 1935. Suddenly caught in the updrafts of a gigantic storm-cloud, they decided to bail out before their planes were shaken to pieces. Alas, the same updraft caught all five parachutes and sent them hurtling several hundred feet higher, into the sky. After a while, they began to descend, only to be caught in another updraft, and so on and so on for several hours. When they finally reached the ground, four of the men had frozen to death.

• ◆ •

THE APPROPRIATELY NAMED KARL WINTER brought his death upon himself in 1984. The 19-year-old poacher had a cunning plan to foil the gamekeepers who tried to follow him through the snowy woods of Rovereda, Switzerland: back-to-front boots. Wearing homemade boots with reversed soles, he hunted without incident, but one day he fell into a crevasse. Search parties set out to find him, went the wrong way, and he died before he could be found.

•◆•

RATHER THAN LOOKING for others, beautiful Ghislaine Sanchez, 37, left Paris for Mont Blanc in October 1990, seeking her inner self. Practicing a form of Buddhist meditation that involves being exposed to extreme cold and standing under freezing waterfalls, she was spotted by climbers as she ran around the mountain. She told them she was trying to prove that enduring temperatures of -30° Fahrenheit would toughen her. But Sanchez wasn't tough enough. A few days later, she was discovered, 6,000 feet up a glacier, having abandoned her clothing altogether, sitting naked in meditation, frozen to death.

For reclusive Joseph Heer, 89, the fatal obsession was money. Compulsively frugal, he cut off power to his Washington, Pennsylvania, home in January 1986. He was found in bed, fully clothed, having died of hypothermia. In an open safe and two steel boxes nearby, police found $200,000 in cash.

IN THE SEVERE WINTER of January 1981, New York City police entered the Bronx apartment of Jessie Smalls, 47, and found her encased in a block of ice. A water pipe had burst and flooded the place, and they had to chop the ice away before they could recover the body.

• ◆ •

LONDONER STEPHEN READER, 25, had been obsessed with the cold for about three years. He had convinced himself that a new Ice Age was coming, and he seemed to be preparing for it. He ate only cold food; if given a hot meal, he would place it in the freezer until it was frozen solid before consuming it. He refused to work anywhere but in freezer centers or at night and insisted on taking his vacations in cold places. In January 1989, he went to Resolute Bay in North Canada, but found it wasn't cold enough for him. After that, he thought about going to Alaska, but somehow ended up in Iceland instead. There he set off for Klanders Mountain, dressed only in a track suit and boots, and with no equipment. He was found five days later at the foot of the mountain, without shoes or socks, lying huddled in a ditch. He had died of exposure and hypothermia. Curiously, he had been institutionalized 10 years prior for arson.

# REVENGE OF THE MACHINES

---

*And now we turn to the malevolence of inanimate objects. Whether it's plain old physics or purposeful vengeance, the machines have it in for us.*

---

DARREN GOOCH, 17, had run away from home after a fight with his parents, and was staying at the Cora Hotel in Euston, England, in early 1988. He boasted to night porter Stanley Rogerson about the way he had purloined three cans of Coca-Cola by tilting the hotel's drink machine. The next night, he tried it again, and the 800-pound machine, perhaps rather put out at being robbed in this way, toppled over on top of him. It took four men to lift the machine off Gooch, but the crushing had caused brain damage, and he died after spending nearly three months in a coma.

Such deaths were widespread in the United States during the 1980s. Either tilted for free drinks or shaken when they failed to produce a can or the right change, the insulted machines struck back, killing 11 American servicemen and injuring 39 more. At least four civilians were canned in a similar fashion.

In March 1992, Russian chess grand master Gudkov outwitted and checkmated a computer three times in a row at a public tournament in Moscow. The next time he touched the machine, it electrocuted him and, though rushed to a hospital, he died.

THE UPWARD ESCALATOR at the New York Telephone Company office, installed in 1974, had a history of problems. In 1982, 30 people were injured when the chain drive broke and the escalator went into reverse, and there had been complaints almost weekly in the months leading to the moment Emma Niskala stepped onto the machine for the last time in September 1987. The 35-year-old clerk had risen a few feet when the step that she was standing on gave way. Swallowed by the escalator, she fell three or four feet into the machinery, the downward motion of the surface steps and the upward motion of those underneath sucking her in. Police tried to free her with their hands and with automobile jacks, but she was crushed to death among the churning gears before they could get her out.

•◆•

EVEN IN THE COUNTRYSIDE, the machines lie in wait. Plastics-factory owner Michael Davis, 53, decided to bore a hole in the garden beside his isolated home at Ranmore Common, England, in April 1991. Instead, he ended up planting himself. He was using a large corkscrew drill attached to a lawn-mowing vehicle, but as he began drilling, his clothes became entangled in the machinery. The soil drill then dug itself into the ground, taking Davis with it. When he was discovered by his wife, Marion, only his head remained unburied. She called the emergency services, but though firemen battled for two hours to rescue the mutilated gardener, they were unable to save his life.

Droppings can be fatal. Construction worker Ramon José Rodriguez, 23, was innocently going about his business at a site in Miami, Florida, in December 1988, when a portable toilet fell off the fourth floor of the building and landed on him. He was pronounced dead an hour later. The toilet was on rollers and was thought to have been blown down in a gust of wind.

PAUL G. THOMAS, 47, was the co-owner of a wool mill in Thompson, Connecticut. In August 1987 he was operating a pinwheel dresser machine, which winds woolen yarn from a large spool onto a smaller one. Somehow he fell onto the small spool and was tightly bound to it as 800 yards of yarn were automatically spun around him. He suffocated before the accident was discovered.

A young employee of the Bennett Food Factory in the Bronx, New York, died instantly when he fell headfirst into an industrial dough mixer making macaroni and was impaled by the mixing blades.

INVENTOR HECTOR PENNA spent four years developing a powerful factory-cooling fan. He was modifying the invention in his laboratory in San Julian, Argentina, when his wife walked in and flicked on the light switch, not realizing that he had connected it to the fan. He was decapitated by the blades.

• ◆ •

SOMETIMES IT SEEMS that the killer machinery has a very specific target. The Prado family was returning by bus to Santa Ana, California, from a trip to Mexico in May 1992. As the bus sped along the San Diego Freeway, four-year-old Ramon fell asleep with his head on his mother's lap. At Oceanside, 70 miles south of Los Angeles, one of the bus's tires blew out. Steel cables from the tire thrashed a three-foot hole through the floor of the bus, and one snaked up, wrapped itself around Ramon, and dragged him down onto the freeway. He was run over by the bus, but no one else was hurt, including the boy's mother.

• ◆ •

THOMAS MAGUIRE OF CAHIR, County Tipperary, Ireland, worked for Shift-It Ltd., a garbage removal company. In January 1993, the 47-year-old arrived at a supermarket to collect a crate full of stale vegetables and garbage, a job he had done regularly for three years. A couple of hours later, the supermarket reported Maguire missing, though his garbage-packing truck was still there, with its motor running. Maguire had been standing on the crate and was sucked into the truck with the rubbish, where he was packed to death as the garbage truck compressed and crushed him.

• ◆ •

ALAS, CLEANLINESS CAN BE a little too close to godliness. In Boston, laundry worker Alfredo Castro, 31, was inspecting a large clothes dryer in January 1991. As he did so, a load of wet laundry dropped on him, pushing him into the machine; the lid slammed shut and the machine started automatically. Castro was trapped in the spinning drum for six minutes and died from suffocation after being tossed around in a temperature of 180° Fahrenheit. His body was eventually spilled out with the laundry, "looking like a boiled lobster."

•◆•

PERHAPS THE MOST LUDICROUS laundry death comes from the western Chinese province of Xinjiang, where two schoolteachers, Aierguma and his wife, Paheerguli, hired a 16-year-old nanny in July 1991. The relatively affluent couple owned a washing machine, and one day during their lunch hour they taught the girl how it worked. Before returning to his job, Aierguma told the young nanny, "After finishing the laundry, don't forget to bathe the baby." She did exactly as she was told; after finishing with the clothes, she put the one-year-old boy in the washing machine and turned on the power. The infant drowned. The teachers were said to "regret hiring an uncultured nanny."

Eighty-year-old Adelaide Magnasco went on vacation to Aosta, Italy, in August 1993. Retiring for the night, she pulled down the Murphy bed from the wall of her chalet, got in it, and died when it suddenly snapped closed. She was found by her son, Paulo, crushed between the mattress and the wall.

# JUST COINCIDENCE?

---◆---

*"It's just coincidence." We've all said it at some time or other, but is there more to it than that? Are there self-replicating events, happenings that try to tell us something by recurring? Do some events start as fiction and later emerge as reality?*

---◆---

LIFE DOES, IN FACT, IMITATE ART. In 1837, Edgar Allan Poe wrote *The Narrative of Arthur Gordon Pym*, in which four shipwrecked and starving sailors drew lots to pick who would be eaten. The loser was named Richard Parker. In 1884, the *Mignonette* was shipwrecked in the southern Atlantic. Three sailors survived for 20 days on two cans of parsnips, a captured turtle, and the fourth sailor, a 17-year-old boy whom the others killed and ate. The survivors were finally rescued and returned to England, where two of them were sentenced to death, but then reprieved. The victim's name was Richard Parker.

◆

IN NEW ORLEANS, MORE THAN 100 lifeguards threw a party in April 1992, to celebrate their first year without a tragedy. While they were busy partying, one of the guests, who was not a lifesaver, fell into the swimming pool fully clothed and drowned, even though four lifeguards were on duty.

OPERA STAR MARIE COLLIER, who came to fame when she stood in for Maria Callas in *Tosca* in 1966, also seemed to be possessed by her character. In the last act of the opera, the heroine leaps to her death. Several years later, during a meeting at her London home with her financial adviser concerning a tour of America, Marie Collier opened a balcony window and fell out, plunging 30 feet to her death in the street below.

•◆•

DOUBLY COINCIDENTAL WAS the death of 65-year-old bingo-caller Michael Cave. He idolized television comedian Tommy Cooper, who died on the air. Cave had been watching television and saw it happen; he told his wife that that was exactly the way *he* wanted to go. In June 1992, Cave was 15 minutes into his bingo routine at a club in Reading, England, when he called "Number eight... Pearly Gates," and then collapsed. He was rushed to the hospital, and was dead on arrival.

•◆•

IN THE VILLAGE OF MOOSBRUN, Austria, the brass band played an annual spring concert that brought with it bad fortune. In 1987, during the "Klevenhuller March," 71-year-old conductor Johann Kolominn collapsed and died onstage of a heart attack. The following year, new conductor Franz Gessner, 70, included the same march in the program, in memory of his predecessor. As the audience watched in horror, the conductor's baton froze in midair and he, too, died of a heart attack.

•◆•

MIKE STEWART, 31, president of the Auto Convoy Company of Dallas, was filming a movie in April 1983 about the traffic dangers of low-level bridges, when the truck he was standing on passed under a suburban bridge and killed him.

THE APTLY NAMED AMELIA SMOKE, 22, was visiting a friend in Chicago in August 1901, and the friend's son was smoking. Picking up a cigarette, Miss Smoke declared: "It is becoming a fad to smoke cigarettes—I will light this one up and take a puff for fun." The fun didn't last. A spark dropped in the folds of her dress, and soon the flames reached her face. She was dead before the fire could be extinguished.

•◆•

ERSKINE LAWRENCE EBBIN was knocked off his moped by a taxi and killed in Hamilton, Ontario, on July 20, 1975. It was the same taxi, with the same driver, carrying the same passenger, that had killed his brother, Neville, on the same day of the previous year. Both brothers were 17 when they died, and had been riding the same moped on the same street. One thing only prevented history from repeating itself precisely: the time of day was 50 minutes different.

•◆•

IN OCTOBER 1987, A PICNIC was held on the banks of the crocodile-infested Zambezi River, in the Caprivi Strip between Botswana and Zambia. As postmaster Kobus Slabbert was warning children to stay out of the water, a giant crocodile grabbed Slabbert by the leg and dragged him, screaming, down the riverbank. He surfaced twice before disappearing, but his corpse was never recovered.

In July 1989, Michael Doucette, 16, from Concord, New Hampshire, was honored as America's safest teenage driver in a contest called "Operation Driver Excellence," held in Detroit. He won a $5,000 scholarship, a trophy and the use of a 1989 Dodge for a year. He was driving the Dodge February 23, 1990, when he crashed head-on with a car driven by Sharon Ann Link, 19. Both were killed. Police said that Doucette appeared to have fallen asleep at the wheel.

SALVATORE AND FLORENCE GRAZIANO hit it off when they met at a Chicago dance in 1932: they married a year later and remained inseparable for more than 50 years. In October 1984, Salvatore, age 77, had a heart attack and was taken to Illinois Masonic Hospital for treatment, where 75-year-old Florence visited him daily. One morning she arrived at the hospital and told a nurse that she wasn't feeling well, so she was taken to a doctor's office for a checkup before seeing her husband. Strangely, Salvatore's condition had deteriorated overnight, and he died while Florence was being examined. At the precise moment of his death, 9:09 a.m., Florence flopped into the doctor's arms and died. She suffered only a mild heart attack, which shouldn't have killed her, and there was no way that she could have known of her husband's death.

•◆•

OF COURSE, THERE ARE OCCASIONS when coincidence seems more like cosmic justice. Vincent Orr, 38, served four years in jail for the New Year's Day 1985 murder of his girlfriend, Gillian Callaghan. Orr admitted to repeatedly hitting Callaghan's head on the concrete floor of their home in Radcliffe, England, following a drinking session and an argument. In the summer of 1991, he went on vacation to Corfu with his new girlfriend. Taking an early morning dip on his first day there, he smashed his head on some rocks and died in the hospital several hours later.

IN AUGUST 1987, an 18-year-old woman from Egham, England, died in the hospital after being crushed under her horse that had collapsed from a stroke. Her name was Jennifer Squelch.

•◆•

ON THE MORNING of November 8, 1995, Vittorio Veroni was killed on the Via Cartoccio level-crossing in Reggio Emilia, northern Italy, when his Renault 21 was hit by a train and carried along the line. His daughter, Cristina, 19, had been killed four years earlier, on January 19, 1991, at the same crossing, by the same train, driven by the same driver. Suggestions that he decided to take his life at the place where his daughter died were repudiated by his family and the train conductor, Domenico Serafino.

•◆•

FIVE MOUNTAIN-RESCUE police officers helping to make a film about the dangers of avalanches in the French Alps were swept away and killed by an avalanche in December 1980. TV cameramen looked on in disbelief, but were unable to prevent the tragedy.

# DOMINO DEATHS

*Naturally, deaths do not always come singly, or even in pairs; all too frequently they cluster in large-scale accidents or even in larger extinctions. But occasionally there are stories in which there seems to be a chain of causation: one death leads to another, and another, and another.*

THE MONTOYA FAMILY had a 13th-floor apartment in the Caballito district of Buenos Aires. They were away in October 1988, but they left their poodle, Cachi, behind. Somehow, Cachi got over the wall of their balcony, which faced the street, and plummeted to his death. He landed on the head of 75-year-old Marta Espina, killing her instantly. A crowd of onlookers gathered around the bodies, including Edith Sola, 46, who was unable to get close and had to stand in the middle of the street. There, Edith was knocked down and killed by a bus. Shocked, an elderly man who had seen both incidents had a heart attack and died in the ambulance on the way to the hospital. A neighbor remarked: "There were bodies everywhere. It looked as if a bomb had exploded."

In the Ukraine, a June 1988 funeral wake turned to drunken revelry and then disaster. The funeral, in the village of Zabolotye, was for a man who had died of poisoning after drinking black-market industrial spirits. The same rotgut was served at the wake, killing 10 guests and hospitalizing 80.

IN THE SORT OF GRIM disaster that happens at least once a year in some part of the world, five farmers followed each other to their death in a manure pit in Menominee, Michigan, in July 1989. Carl Theuerkauf, 65, his sons Carl Jr. and Tom, grandson Daniel and friend Bill Hofer were attempting to clear a drain in the 13-foot manure pit, which was a foot deep in dung at the time. Hofer went in first and collapsed as he was overcome by the colorless, odorless methane gas given off by the manure. One of the Theuerkaufs went in to save him and was also overcome. Then the others followed, one after another, until all five were killed, leaving only Theuerkauf's third son, Bill, who had already been badly injured in a car accident three years previously, to run the dairy farm.

• ◆ •

IN AN ATTEMPT TO RESCUE a chicken on July 31, 1996, farmer's son Allam Sabet al-Sayyed, 18, descended a 60-foot-deep well in the Egyptian village of Nazlat Imara, 240 miles south of Cairo. He drowned, apparently after an undercurrent pulled him down. When he failed to appear, his brother Sayyed, 20, climbed down to investigate, and he, too, drowned. Then their brother Ahmad, 16, descended and vanished—to be followed by their 14-year-old sister, Zeinab. Two elderly cousins arrived to see if they could help, but suffered the same fate. The bodies of all six were later pulled out, along with the chicken, the only survivor.

• ◆ •

OCCASIONALLY, DEATH SEEMS to have a particular attachment to a place, visiting again and again. The sleepy village of Woodseaves, England, with a population of only 500, was such a place, shaken by a series of fatal accidents and bizarre suicides in 1989–90. Vicar Roy Harrison was the latest victim, hanging himself in the stairwell of his vicarage in November 1990, shortly after the death of his mother. A week earlier, factory worker Darren Holmes had gone to his former lover's house and burned himself to death. The previous month, fencing contractor Ray Langham died when he crashed his Jaguar. Before that, John Clapham, a fruit and vegetable merchant from the village, was killed on a business trip to California, when he was hit by a truck after his car broke down. A few months earlier still, Roy Lawrence died of kidney failure when he was given the wrong type of blood during surgery. And finally, weapons expert Gerald Bliss was testing a "fail-safe" weapons system for the Ministry of Defense when he was killed by an exploding shell. The village postmistress remarked: "It's as if there's a curse on the place."

• ◆ •

AND SPEAKING OF CURSES, consider the following tale. On August 30, 1990, Simon Craven, 28, was fatally injured when his car collided with two parked vehicles on the Eastbourne seafront. He was the eighth Earl of Craven, and his death was the latest in a series of events that seemed to fulfill a 350-year-old curse on the family, supposedly the work of a pregnant servant. The first Earl was William Craven, a soldier who received the title in 1626. Since then, no Earl has lived beyond the age of 57. Simon Craven's elder brother, Thomas, the seventh Earl, shot himself in 1983 in a fit of depression, at age 26. His father died at 47 from leukemia. His grandfather died at 35 during a wild party on a yacht. Although the family is said not to believe in the curse, it is also thought to center on the Craven ancestral home, Morewood House in Berkshire, which was sold after the seventh Earl's suicide. The latest owner of the house, Dr. Robert Reid, committed suicide shortly before Simon Craven's death.

In August 1984, Vebi Limani was struck dead by lightning near his home on Sara Mountain in southern Yugoslavia. His father, one of his brothers and an uncle had suffered the same fate in recent years, while his sister was permanently injured by a lightning bolt.

WE CONCLUDE WITH the credibility-stretching tale of artist Hans Kinnow from Budapest. In the late 1930s, he painted a portrait of a millionaire's wife. He'd just finished it when his model slumped dead of heart failure. His next sitter was a wealthy bank director, who died a few days after his picture was completed, and the next subject, the daughter of a doctor, died too. Kinnow vowed never to paint again, but a year later he fell in love. Just before he and his fiancée were to be married, he agreed to paint her portrait; she died of pneumonia within a week. Kinnow became an odd-job man, and was found dead in a cheap Budapest lodging house in April 1938. Beside him was a crayon sketch dated the previous day—of himself.

# TAKE TWO

*From tales where death strikes repeatedly, we move on to those where the Grim Reaper misses with his first shot but improves his aim with the second. Are the near-misses dress rehearsals?*

LEBANESE-BORN AIR STEWARD Mohammed Wafiq Zarif and his English wife, Kathleen Denham, divorced in 1985 but remained friends. Shortly before returning to Lebanon in December 1990, Zarif took out 12 life insurance policies worth $1.65 million; four days after his arrival in Beirut, he was reported killed in a car crash. Apparently acting in good faith, Denham went ahead and submitted a claim on the policies, as well as on his British Airways pension. But the death was faked, and in January 1991, Zarif phoned his ex-wife. She later told police that Zarif had threatened to have her murdered by a friend if she didn't press ahead with the claims, but as the insurance companies couldn't get confirmation of his death from Lebanon, only one of the policies was paid. Denham obtained $22,500, of which she sent $15,000 to Zarif. He went out and bought a car with his ill-gotten gains, and in July 1991 he crashed it—this time, however, he was killed.

Ioannis Philippou, 50, accidentally set himself on fire while huddled over a heater in his home in Kato Deftera, Cyprus, in January 1990. To douse the flames, he ran out of the house and jumped into a reservoir, where he drowned.

IN BRENTWOOD, ENGLAND, a 25-year-old named Charles Millbank crashed his automobile into an electricity pole on the freeway, in January 1993. The car plunged over an embankment, but Milbank escaped unhurt. As he scrambled back up the slope, however, he touched the 11,000-volt cable trailing across the grass and was killed instantly.

•◆•

IN FEBRUARY 1983, a fierce gust of wind blew Vittorio Luise's car into the River Sele near Naples, Italy. Luise, 45, managed to break a window, climb out and swim to shore. There a tree blew down and killed him.

•◆•

IN JULY 1991, 65-year-old Chan Wai-fong set up a small shrine at her son's home in Hong Kong to give thanks to the gods for her daughter's lucky escape from a road accident. As she was praying in the street outside the apartment block, she was killed by a falling bag of cement.

•◆•

WOODROW KREEKMORE had a narrow escape in February 1985 when his car skidded off an icy road and slammed into a telegraph pole outside Chickasha, Oklahoma. He climbed out and strolled into the road to hitch a ride, but had only walked a couple of feet when behind him the pole toppled over and struck him dead.

IN THE PHILIPPINES, Enrique Quinanola, 21 and unemployed, tried to hang himself at his home in Cebu City on September 11, 1990. His relatives cut the rope and took him to the hospital. As doctors prepared to sedate him he escaped, ran to a nearby restaurant, grabbed a knife and slashed his wrists. Police saw the incident and tried to subdue him, but he put up such a struggle that they shot him, first in the leg and then in the chest. He died a few moments later. Astonishingly, Quinanola's family then filed a complaint with the government's Human Rights Commission, alleging that his civil liberties had been violated.

•◆•

GEORGE SCHWARTZ, 54, was alone and working late in the office of his factory in Providence, Rhode Island, in December 1983. A huge explosion virtually flattened the building and sent flames racing through the wreckage. Only one wall was left standing, but the blast swept Schwartz clear of falling masonry and flames, dumping him on the front steps. After treatment for minor injuries and shock, he returned to the factory to try to salvage his business files, whereupon the last remaining wall collapsed and killed him.

Convicted murderer Michael Godwin, 28, avoided the electric chair in Columbia, South Carolina, when his sentence was reduced to life imprisonment on appeal. In March 1988, he was sitting naked on the metal commode in his cell, trying to mend the headphones on his TV. He bit through a wire and was electrocuted.

Rose Knox strangled her eight-year-old son in 1953 and was sentenced to hang. The penalty was commuted and she spent seven years in jail. She remarried in 1965, but was often depressed about her former actions. In February 1981, she committed suicide at age 60 in her home in Chester-le-Street, Durham, England. She overdosed on drugs and hanged herself with a washing line in a bedroom doorway.

•◆•

In August 1977, an unnamed man went fishing on the banks of the Rio Negro in Amazonia. His fishing line caught in a tree, and as he tried to free it, he struck a bees' nest. The infuriated swarm went on the attack, and to escape, the man leapt into the river, where he was devoured by piranhas.

# NATURAL
# SELECTION

———◆———

*There are many ways in which one can be
responsible for one's own death: an act of
stupidity, a plan that goes wrong, a long-
held obsession. In the following stories, the
survival instinct seems to be on vacation.*

———◆———

NITARO ITO, 41, a restaurant owner from Osaka, Japan, ran
for election to the House of Representatives in 1979. Hoping to generate free publicity and voter sympathy by running his campaign from a hospital bed, he asked friends to
beat him up, and then he stabbed himself in the thigh.
Unfortunately, he died from loss of blood during the 20-
yard walk from his car to his house.

●◆●

A POACHER, ELECTROCUTING fish in a Polish lake, died when
he fell into the water and suffered the same fate as his quarry.
The 24-year-old man was one of four who had attached a
cable to a fishing net and a high-voltage electricity line.

●◆●

KENNETH SUTHERLAND, a 38-year-old autoworker from
Sumpter Township, Michigan, had a nice little sideline
growing marijuana plants in his garage. The only trouble was
that the local teenagers occasionally broke in and stole them.
Sutherland eventually decided to rig up a booby trap. He

nailed a shotgun to a chair and ran a wire from the trigger to an outer screen door, so that the gun would go off if the door was opened. One day in June 1993, he made a fatal mistake: he forgot about his own trap. The shotgun blasted him in the thigh, and though he managed to drag himself the 60 feet to his house and dial an ambulance, he was then unable to say anything. He bled to death before help could arrive.

• ◆ •

FLORIAN IORGA, 42, and his son, Aurel, 16, had a similar difficulty in remembering the whereabouts of a booby trap they had set up—this time to protect their onion patch in Bucharest, Romania. Hearing noises in the night, they ran out to investigate—and tripped over the cables they had wired to the mains around the perimeter of the patch. The bodies were found by Iorga's wife.

• ◆ •

WHEN STEPHEN SMITH was 11, he saw his mother survive a heart attack. In the years that followed, he became more and more obsessed with death, despite his mother's attempts to persuade him that he was worrying needlessly. He would burst into tears and tell of dreams in which he was lying in a coffin while his friends and relatives stood around it, crying. Finally, in October 1983, at the age of 19, Stephen collapsed for no discernible reason and died of heart failure. Relatives were convinced that he had been so terrified of dying that he had scared himself to death.

• ◆ •

POLISH-BORN KAZIMERZ SYMANSKI was a prisoner in World War II, and never got over the experience. He turned his flat in north London into a cell, placing bars on the windows and sleeping in a wooden box in the form of a cage that had a grilled door he could chain shut from the inside. The flat was even more like a prison camp in that it had neither electricity nor running water, and he used the kitchen floor as a toilet. The windows were nailed open because he feared being gassed; he also suspected he was being attacked by radiation, he reported to a neighbor. Symanski, 81, was thought to have lived in these conditions for five years. When police eventually broke down his barricaded front door in April 1993, they found that the conditions, and the open windows, had got the better of the old man: he had died of bronchial pneumonia, caused by hypothermia.

• ◆ •

MASAHIRO OKI, 64, was a grand master in Japanese martial arts and an expert on yoga. He held three degrees in Western medicine, and others in Oriental medicine, and was reputed to be the only samurai not to have prostrated himself before Emperor Hirohito, even though Oki had once been the emperor's personal physician. He and his students had moved to Pesaro, Italy, where he continued his yogic practices. Oki was said to have attained a level in which the four elements are regarded as a form of illusion. In August 1985, he began to meditate on this by wearing a lead-weighted jacket and assuming the lotus position underwater. He drowned during his fourth immersion, and his students were unable to resuscitate him, despite using ancient "samurai" methods.

• ◆ •

JOHN BUTTERICK, A RESEARCHER at West Virginia University, was obsessed with extending the human life span. While studying in Canada, he had spent six months ingesting BHT, a chemical used in food packaging to retard spoiling. Later, he believed he had found the miracle chemical that would allow him to live for 200 years: warfarin, a pharmaceutical drug sometimes used in small quantities as an anticoagulant but best known for its use as rat poison. In January 1980, he was found lying on his bed in his apartment having bled to death, with blood covering his clothes, the mattress, a glass, the kitchen floor and the bathroom. His quest for immortality had been cut short at the age of 33.

•◆•

NO ONE REALLY KNOWS what Arthur Sharland was getting out of it, but his turn-on was electricity. The 77-year-old retiree from Shepherd's Bush, London, would sit in an armchair with two wires running from an electric socket to crocodile clips that he attached to his bare chest before flicking on the power. In August 1989, he was found fatally electrocuted, although the mass of tiny scars on his chest, some of which were many years old, suggested that he'd been plugging himself in for much of his life.

In Mexico, it may be routine to swallow worms with tequila, but on the U.S. West Coast an unnamed 29-year-old man went one better in 1979. Having drunk half a pint of whiskey, he then swallowed a newt on a dare. Unfortunately, he chose to swallow a newt of the *taricha granulosa* family, which is a hundred times more poisonous than its East Coast cousins, and contains enough toxin to kill 1,500 white mice. He died a few hours later.

HARRY DORRAN, 31, and his brother, Steve, 21, both from Henstridge, England, proved to be even more stupidly daring. After a fishing trip they decided to play "chicken" by lying down in the middle of a dark road. As they dared their friends to join them, a car ran over them. Harry was killed, while Steve was hospitalized with serious head and leg injuries.

• ◆ •

EVEN THE LESS INTREPID have delusions of grandeur. Forty-six-year-old school principal Bernard Golden of Amherstburg, Ontario, Canada, turned into a cowboy in the evenings. Strapping on a low-slung Western-style holster and holding a stopwatch, he practiced gun tricks with a .35 Magnum pistol in front of the mirror at his home. In March 1980, he was going over his gun spin, but this time all six chambers of the revolver were fully loaded. The gun went off and he died, having fatally shot himself in the chest.

• ◆ •

WALTER HALLAS OF LEEDS, England, thought he was a pretty tough guy, but was terrified of going to the dentist. Tormented by a toothache in November 1979, he decided on a cowboy-style cure, and asked workmate Mark Waldron to knock the tooth out by punching him on the jaw. After some hesitation, Waldron duly obliged with a right jab, whereupon Hallas, 26, fell to the ground and hit his head with a loud crack on the concrete floor. He died in a hospital six days later, of a fractured skull.

• ◆ •

ON HALLOWEEN 1988, Michael Tyree turned up at a bar in Boston, Massachusetts, dressed in a spooky costume and with a noose in hand. As a prank, 41-year-old Tyree wanted to stage a fake hanging, but the bar owner wouldn't let him. He left, but returned an hour later when the owner had gone for the night, and proceeded with his stunt. Something went wrong with his harness, and he began choking to death before a group of delighted revelers who had no idea he was dying before their eyes. He was eventually cut down and rushed to a hospital, but couldn't be saved.

WE FEEL A CERTAIN SENSE of satisfaction when the subversion of a venerable institution is punished. Spanish police had given the nickname "Santa Claus" to the burglar who had made 12 successful raids on Pyrenean ski lodges, since his method of entry was to slide down old-fashioned chimneys while the lodges were locked up for the summer. In 1985, on his thirteenth caper, things went wrong for Jo Montpol, age 26. He slid down a chimney in Viella, but got stuck in an extractor fan and starved to death.

In July 1977, a man was knocked down by a car in New York, but he got up uninjured. A bystander told him to lie down in front of the car again and pretend he was hurt so that he could collect some insurance money. He did, and the car promptly rolled forward and crushed him to death.

DEREK CHARLES, OF BRIXTON, ENGLAND, was too shy to consult a doctor about his incontinence, so in November 1987 he tried to cure himself by wrapping an elastic band tightly around his penis. The "cure" caused kidney failure, and he died as a result.

• ◆ •

LOUISE RAMOS, 64, was arrested for shoplifting in San Diego, California, in October 1983. Protesting, she vowed to hold her breath "until I turn blue." True to her word, that's exactly what she did, and died in the hospital a few days later.

BROTHER CONSTANTINO was an extremely devout monk, who beat his head on the hard pew in front of him as he prayed in a monastery in southern Italy. In June 1987, he carried devotion too far, banged his head more rigorously than usual, and killed himself.

RAYMOND PRIESTLEY OF MELBOURNE, Australia, wanted to try the snooker shot of a lifetime in January 1979. He suspended himself over the table, hanging by his legs from the rafters, but he slipped, crashed headfirst onto the concrete floor and died.

# SUICIDE IS PAINFUL

---•◆•---

*People decide to kill themselves for many peculiar reasons, but the ways in which they choose to do it are often stranger still.*

---•◆•---

CORY QUINN, FROM SYDNEY, Australia, committed suicide by locking himself in his estranged wife's freezer when she went on vacation. He left a note for the 280-pound woman that said: "Gorge on this, you fat pig!"

•◆•

IN EAST LONDON, SOUTH AFRICA, a crowd of bystanders gathered in 1979 to watch as a man stood at the top of cliff, threatening to throw himself over the edge. As he teetered indecisively, a 64-year-old man stepped forward from the crowd, announced that he would show him how it was done, and promptly plunged to his death. The first man was so startled and horrified that he fainted and was dragged clear by onlookers.

•◆•

JILTED LOVER SCOTT MCCRAW, 37, from Long Island, New York, committed suicide on February 21, 1994, by agitating Shakey, his pet rattlesnake, until it bit him. He died of heart failure in a field, while the snake died of hypothermia. The bodies were not discovered for 19 days.

APTLY NAMED SANDRA KILLINGTON, 21, of Barking, England, was either obsessed with the past or the past was obsessed with her. According to her diary, she had fallen in love with a merchant named Thomas Fanshawe who had lived in the 1600s, believing that he was somehow still alive and having a relationship with her in 1981. She wrote in her diary: "I'm going to kill myself so we can go back to live as we used to." Then she lay down in front of a train while holding her four-year-old daughter, Nicola. Nicola struggled free of her mother's arms at the last moment; Sandra, however, died for her strange love.

• ◆ •

A CITROËN WAS THE OBJECT of 22-year-old Michael Bennett's passion. One night in 1991, he overturned it on the way back from the pub to his home in Driffield, Humberside, England. A friend, following in another car, helped him right it and tow it home. Bennett was in tears and kicked the car, then went down on his knees to kiss it, sobbing "Sorry, car." Then he reportedly said: "I want hanging for that." And he meant it: he was found several hours later dangling from a tree, on the same tow rope he'd used to bring the car home.

In March 1981, an unnamed man was found hanging from a tree in Los Angeles. A car was parked nearby, bearing the license plate "Black Dog," and a leather whip was draped over the tree branch. The man was dressed entirely in black, including a black felt hood. He was also wearing a Frankenstein-monster mask.

SOME PEOPLE ARE MORE METHODICAL, to the point of mania. There have been several "suicide machines," but one of the most complex and foolproof was built in 1973 by an unnamed 27-year-old electrician in Auckland, New Zealand. He erected a platform inside his house, with snap locks on chains and wooden crossbars, so that once he was on it he couldn't escape, even if he changed his mind. Above this was an automatic .22-caliber rifle, aimed through a hole in a wooden board suspended directly above his heart. The trigger was connected to a solenoid, which in turn was connected to an electromagnet, two time clocks and two doors. If one clock failed, the other was there as backup; if anyone entered the room, opening the door would also set off the mechanism. And, in case of a power failure, the electromagnet would switch off and pull the trigger. Finally, the man cleared the house thoroughly, emptied and switched off the refrigerator, and left a note for the milkman, telling him not to leave any milk but to call the police. Then he took sleeping pills and locked himself on the platform. He was found dead the next morning with six bullets in his heart.

•◆•

IN TORONTO, CANADA, Franco Brun, 22, turned the very item that was supposed to help him through his troubles into a fast ticket out of them. In 1987, Brun was rushed to the hospital from the detention center where he was serving a 15-day sentence. The authorities had provided him with a pocket Bible the size of a deck of cards, and he had promptly swallowed it. It became so firmly lodged in his throat that doctors could only peel off individual pages rather than remove the whole thing. A tracheotomy was performed, opening his windpipe, but by then it was too late. If Brun didn't go to the grave with the words of the Good Book on his lips, at least he had them in his mouth.

EVEN MORE INVOLVED with Christian religious matters was William Robins of Romford, England, who'd internalized the teachings until he was convinced he was Jesus Christ. On July 2, 1988, dressed only in his underpants, he spent an hour and a half balanced on a rail of the Mercantile Credit building in Holborn, chanting, "God give me strength" and telling onlookers that "I screwed up my mission the first time around, and this time I'm going to get it right." He continued, "If I die today I will rise up and be the second Christ. If I don't die today I will become the Devil." Then he jumped, falling 11 floors and departing this life with multiple injuries.

> Fifty-one peasant girls seeking a second chance committed suicide in 15 separate group drownings in Jiangxi province, China in 1988. Many of the despairing teenagers dressed in their best clothes before jumping in order to present a good image to the gods of the other-world. They were hoping to be reincarnated as rich, sophisticated city women.

STRANGER STILL, THERE WERE mass suicides by pensioners, also concerned about their future in the afterlife, in Jiangsu province, China, in March 1993. According to Chinese tradition, the dead must be buried in order to arrive in the otherworld whole, but the local government decreed that anyone dying after April 1 should be cremated. More than a hundred old people killed themselves to ensure burial, popping sleeping pills, drowning and hanging themselves, and jumping off bridges. One pharmacist reported that a group of pensioners invaded his premises demanding sleeping pills, because they had to beat the deadline. When he told them he'd sold out, they head-butted his drug cabinet before rushing into the street and throwing themselves in front of a passing truck. And one man who tried to gas himself started a house fire and ended up being cremated anyway.

●◆●

IN 1993, IN HENAN PROVINCE, China, four 13-year-olds decided to take a "tour of Hell" after watching a Taiwanese occult soap opera called *New Tales of the White Maiden*. Leaving a suicide note saying, "If Hell is no better than Earth, we will return," they ate a watermelon laced with rat poison. Two died, two survived.

●◆●

A GUATEMALAN GUN SALESMAN committed suicide by hurling himself into a pit of jaguars in Guatemala City's zoo, after accidentally shooting a customer to death. Paco Cazanga, 32, was rescued from the pit by firefighters who used fire extinguishers to repel four jaguars, but he died later in the hospital.

●◆●

ANDREA RUGA, 47, had the same name, birthplace and date of birth as a Mafia godfather accused of terrorism and various kidnappings. Italy's police computers couldn't tell them apart, and the "impeccably honest" hardware merchant from Monasterace in southern Italy constantly had his house raided. At roadblocks, his wife and children sat weeping as he was hustled off to have his papers checked. At hotels, he suffered countless indignities as staff called the police.

On October 24, 1995, he was found dead after taking poison in a road turnoff near Naples. Minutes before, he had phoned three senators, three magistrates, a newspaper editor and the local police chief to say that he couldn't stand the aggravation anymore.

# JUST FOLLOWING ORDERS

---◆---

*"The Devil made me do it." An excuse is always at hand when we act out of character, but sometimes it does seem like there's an invisible Mephistopheles whispering in our ears. Is it only the mad who hear the words, or are we puppets whose strings are pulled by entities somewhere in the great beyond?*

---◆---

GLORIA GONZALES, a 14-year-old girl from Poteet, Texas, was shot dead in February 1981, and Ruben Gonzales Estrada was soon arrested for her murder. Estrada had an excuse, however: God and the Martians were to blame. Nineteen year-old Estrada told the officers who arrested him that he was "ordered by God to do this work" and that he had "five more to go" to complete the assignment. Obviously more than a little confused, he later changed his story, saying, "The Martians made me do it."

●◆●

ANOTHER SPACE CADET WAS Lester Donaldson of Toronto, who believed for years that he was being controlled by aliens. He was referred to Dr. Joseph Johnson, a psychiatrist, to whom he revealed that he had had direct contact with the aliens, and that they'd used "flying-saucer rays" to put a computer in his brain. Johnson diagnosed Donaldson as a paranoid schizophrenic and prescribed drugs, then lost track of the patient for two years. When Donaldson turned up again, this time accompanied by his wife, Myrtle, he claimed that the CIA was controlling him; Myrtle apparently believed his every word, and could not be persuaded otherwise. Donaldson received some treatment but declined the follow-up day care. Eventually, in August 1988, the 44-year-old Donaldson took a knife and attacked police who came by his home. They shot him dead.

Firmly convinced that her husband, Felix, had become possessed by the cartoon character Mickey Mouse, Roseann Greco, 52, killed Felix by repeatedly running him over with her car in the driveway of their home in West Islip, New York. She was convicted of manslaughter and sentenced to 5 to 15 years.

FORMER ENGLISH NAVAL OFFICER Peter Dowdeswell, 60, suffered from periodic bouts of religious obsession after being told 25 years earlier by a naval chaplain that he had been selected for a "spiritual purpose." In January 1979, he received two messages from God. The first came as he and his wife, Marie, were driving home to Eastbourne after a holiday in Ireland: God told him to go to Windsor to see the Queen. When Marie objected, he pushed her out of the car and continued on his own. She was picked up by another motorist and taken to Uxbridge police station. Eventually, Dowdeswell arrived at Windsor Castle and presented himself at the police house, saying he had received a message from God "on the direct line" and that he had a divine duty to save the Queen. Forewarned by their colleagues at Uxbridge, the Windsor police arranged for him to be reunited with his wife at the Castle Hotel, where they took a room.

There Dowdeswell received his second message. He began by trying to convert Marie, apparently because she was obsessed with worldly goods. Then God told him to kill her. He strangled her, and then forced tissues and water down her throat to symbolize the body and blood of Christ, after which he phoned the police and gave himself up. He told detectives he had asked God, "'Do I really have to kill her? Is this my duty?' He said it was my duty." Dowdeswell pleaded guilty to manslaughter.

One can of shaving cream contains enough chemicals to kill a man, but Herbert Pickney didn't want to take any chances. The 38-year-old born-again Christian, serving time in jail at Charleston, South Carolina, ate five cans, then followed them up with eight bars of soap. Before expiring, he confided to guards, "The Lord told me to do it."

IN SHEFFIELD LAKE, OHIO, 23-year-old Michael Trofimov joined a religious group in 1988. Not long afterward, he announced that Christ was in him, and he began to speak in tongues. This didn't seem to straighten out his life, however, or improve his driving—he managed to crash his car into a railway train. He escaped with minor injuries, but shortly thereafter went into convulsions. Taken to the hospital by the uncle with whom he was living at the time, he refused all medication. The next night, after Michael had agreed that attending the religious meetings might not be a good idea, his father came to visit him. All seemed well, and before his uncle and aunt went out for a cup of coffee, Michael told everyone how much he loved them. When they returned, they found Michael talking in tongues and screaming for God ... and strangling his father, John. The elder Trofimov didn't survive. Michael pleaded not guilty to murder by reason of insanity.

In China, three sons consulted a local sorcerer about their 76-year-old father's illness, and were told that the old man's feverish ravings meant that he was possessed by evil spirits. They believed the explanation, and buried their father alive.

CLAUDIA VERNICCI WAS attending the burial of her husband in Florence, Italy, in August 1987, when she heard his voice coming from the coffin. Rather than being the sign of a miraculous resurrection, it turned out that the voice was actually being thrown by ventriloquist Paulo Dino, 32. Dino, who had been trying to break into show business, said, "I only meant it as a joke. I never really thought Mrs. Vernicci would think it was her husband speaking. I thought she'd get a good laugh from it." Dino's sense of humor was misplaced, to say the least; Mrs. Vernicci keeled over, clutching her heart, and died of shock. Dino was arrested.

# CULT MADNESS

*If individuals can perform strange acts under the influence of direct messages from the beyond, then it's hardly surprising that even more weirdness crops up in the hothouse atmosphere of cults, sects and even full-scale religions.*

RODRIGO MANEJA, 33, of Cebu in the Philippines, headed a cult called Kahal ha Masiyac, which believes it will survive a nuclear war. In August 1985, he gathered hundreds of followers and spectators to demonstrate that he could return from the dead within four hours. His brother-in-law poured gasoline over him and ignited it, as Maneja called out to the crowd that "Elohim will protect me." When four hours had passed with no signs of returning life, police took Maneja's charred remains to a funeral parlor. This doesn't suggest much hope for surviving nuclear catastrophe, but Maneja's mother said she would "continue worshipping the God who asked my son to sacrifice his life."

Villagers in the Philippines cut off the heads of a religious leader and his wife in May 1979, after challenging them to prove there was life after death.

KEITH HAIGLER AND HIS WIFE, Kate, seized a bus full of passengers at Jasper, Arkansas, in July 1982. They were members of a cult led by "the Messiah," of which the reports give few details, and they wanted to draw attention to their religion, threatening to shoot passengers unless a TV crew was sent to cover the action. Cameras were rushed to the scene by helicopter, and the Haiglers announced that they were going to kill themselves but their religious faith would enable them to be resurrected after three days. As police ordered them to drop their weapons while thousands watched the live broadcast, Haigler appeared to be preparing to shoot his wife. She moved first, however, and shot him in the head, then turned the gun on herself. Three days passed, but there was no resurrection.

• ◆ •

AN EVEN LARGER EVENT occurred in February 1992, when two million people gathered around the sacred lake of Kumbakonam, near Madras in the southern Indian state of Tamil Nadu, seeking to wash away their sins. Forty-seven people were killed, some when a wall they were standing on collapsed under their weight; the rest were trampled to death by a stampeding crowd. Some witnesses explained that the stampede resulted from the crowd pressing forward to bathe during the 45 minutes that astrologers had designated as particularly auspicious. Others had a stranger tale to tell: The state's chief minister, Jayalalitha, who had played the roles of Hindu gods in popular films before turning to politics, was present, and the crowd had stampeded for a glimpse of him taking a ritual bath.

• ◆ •

A "GODMAN" IN INDIA called Khadeshwari Baba claimed yogic powers and announced that he would enter a 10-foot-deep pit near the town hall in Gorakhpur on October 20, 1980, and remain there in deep meditation before emerging alive after ten days. District officials were present when he entered the pit, and something of a show was arranged around the event by another yogi called Pilot Baba. More than 1,000 people, mostly women, gathered around the pit, making offerings of cash, gold and valuables worth several thousand rupees, all of which mysteriously vanished along with Pilot Baba at the end of the affair. The ten days passed, and Khadeshwari failed to emerge from the pit. A man was lowered in to find out what had happened, and he reported an overpowering stench; Khadeshwari had been dead for several days.

A snake appeared under a peepul tree in Hapur, near Delhi, India, in February 1992, and was taken by Hindus as divine sanction for plans to build a temple at the site. A group of Muslims objected, and the ensuing street battle left eight dead. The snake, however, left the scene as soon as the clash erupted.

KRZYSZTOF AZNINSKI, 30, had been drinking all day in his garden in Poland with three friends. The four men put on traditional "toughness bonnets" and played macho games. Franciszek Zyzcoszusko, 41, put his hand on a chopping block and dared Azninski to cut it off. Azninski hacked at it with a knife, partially severing the wrist, then put his own head on the block and challenged Zyzcoszusko to chop it off—which he did, with an ax. The revelers then decided things had gone too far, stopped the contest and began to sing a folk song called "Roll the Head of the Giant," which woke the neighbors.

THE COMEDIAN WHO CHOKED ON A PIE...

In Tanzania, nine youths who were members of the Pathfinders, a scoutlike organization, were in a canoe on Lake Victoria on their way to a religious festival on an island. They were accompanied by a Seventh-day Adventist cleric and were part of a flotilla making the October 1993 journey. According to witnesses, they decided to prove their faith by walking on the water, and in the process ten of them drowned.

IN DECEMBER 1975, the body of Jean-Paul Maurice, 20, was found beneath the walls of the Dinant citadel, an old fortress in Belgium. He was assumed to have died of natural causes, and was duly buried. However, in February 1976, Michel Piersotte, 21, was found dead near another fortress, Namur Castle, and an examination showed that his internal organs had been crushed "by an amazing force." Noting the similarities in the place of death, and discovering that both young men had been members of the California sect Children of God, founded in 1968, the police decided to exhume Maurice's body. They discovered that he had died in exactly the same way as Piersotte, and that both men had expressed a desire to leave the sect; details of their deaths remain a mystery.

•◆•

THREE WOMEN, LED BY ALEXANDRA SILVIA, caused an outbreak of collective madness on the island of Faaite in French Polynesia shortly after their arrival in August 1987. They claimed to represent the Catholic charismatic renewal movement, which had a strong following among the island's

180-strong population, and promptly took over the small church and replaced the lay preacher as the source of religious authority. Silvia, conducting the services in trance, told islanders that God would abandon Faaite, that demons were in their midst and that those who failed to attend the daily service were open to suspicion. The three women left the island, having designated seven devoted followers as their disciples. Exorcisms were carried out to rid the devil-possessed. On September 2, Assistant Mayor Ioane Harris denounced the movement.

Harris was pronounced possessed, and maddened villagers twisted a cord around his neck, held a crucifix before his face and beat him senseless. He was then drowned in a ritual in the lagoon, and the body was thrown on a bonfire. Five more people were killed in the next two days. One, a mentally retarded young man who claimed to be Jesus Christ, was burned alive. Another man was strangled and then burned, and his wife was hurled alive into the flames. Order was eventually restored on September 4, when a police squad arrived just in time to prevent four further executions, and 24 islanders were charged with murder.

• ◆ •

IN MAY 1987, Sun Yingpeng started a "sacred sect" in eastern China, saying he was looking for a select band to travel to paradise. Sun, from Lixin county in Anhui province, enrolled six others, and they assembled on a riverbank to wait for a magic boat to come and take them to paradise. They sang and danced, but the boat failed to appear, so the group walked into the river, where six drowned. Hong Yinglao, whose husband and daughter-in-law were among the dead, was rescued by fishermen. As the only survivor, she said later: "I won't do this kind of thing again."

# BLACK MAGIC

---•◆•---

*If magic works, you might think practition-
ers would use their powers to protect
themselves. Alas, tales of invulnerable
witches and magicians are few
and far between.*

---•◆•---

THE SMALL VILLAGE OF HESLOUP in Normandy, France,
was one of those farming communities where many things
had remained unchanged since the Middle Ages, including
the tradition of local wizards. Since adolescence Michel
Herisson had been using magic to cure illnesses and to
improve the yield of crops and livestock. But the man the
villagers really admired was old Jules Camus, who they
thought had far greater supernatural powers than Michel.
Surprisingly, on his deathbed in 1973 Jules passed on his
powers to Michel rather than to his own son, Jean. After
that, a war of the wizards broke out.

Things started to go wrong for the Herisson family.
Their barley crop failed and their vineyard dried up, the
cattle developed strange diseases and had to be destroyed.
Michel's brother Eugene dropped dead of a heart attack,
although he had no previous record of illness. His sister,
Louisette, and a cousin both had road accidents. And when
the villagers began to accuse Jean Camus of having the evil
eye and of causing misery by sticking pins in photographs

of his victims, he seems to have accepted the blame, and rejoiced in the title they gave him: the Beast.

The stories had it that Jean had killed the village policeman's three small children with a curse, and that when the distraught father had tried to shoot the wizard, the bullet had turned back and hit the policeman's own ear. Michel's elder brother, Daniel, claimed that Jean had predicted that Daniel would be killed by a shotgun blast, and shortly thereafter he had wounded himself with his own gun. Obviously, Jean was to blame for everything, and no amount of magic seemed to stop him.

Finally, Michel and Daniel decided something had to be done. One night in March 1976, they walked the mile to Jean's tiny cottage and roused him from a drunken stupor. Telling him that he was a more powerful witch doctor, Michel turned Jean's own prediction back on him by blasting him in the head with a shotgun, and this time no amount of protective magic could save him. In the next few days, the sun came out and the crops began to grow again, but Michel and Daniel couldn't enjoy the improvement. They were in jail.

> Two witch doctors in Zimbabwe who claimed they could cure AIDS have died from the disease after having sex with patients they believed they had cured.

WHEN SHE WAS 17, Madeleine Baumgartner had suffered from excruciating headaches, which doctors had been unable to cure. In desperation, her mother went to see Madame Delamare, a "psychic healer" who asked for 100 francs a month, a lock of the girl's hair and a photograph of her. Delamare said she'd call the spirits to help. Amazingly, it seemed to work, and Madeleine got on with her life, marrying a hotel owner in Paris. Then, in 1976, Madeleine's mother died, and the headaches returned. By April 1978, 44-year-old Madeleine had deduced that it must be because the payments had stopped, so she hired a taxi to take her to Madame Delamare's flat. While the taxi waited outside for 25 minutes, she stabbed the old woman more than a hundred times, then calmly took the cab back to her husband's hotel. For some reason, she told the driver "I have just killed someone." He believed her, and informed the police, who tracked down both murderer and victim. Searching Madame Delamare's flat, they found over 200 envelopes, each containing either a photo or a lock of hair, or both, which, at 100 francs a month each, represented a tidy income. Madeleine's headaches disappeared and she was feeling much better, but she ended up in jail.

•◆•

A RASH OF WITCH BURNINGS and killings in northern South Africa erupted in January 1984. At the beginning of the month, police arrested 18 villagers at Molethlane after a man and woman were burned alive, and in the following four weeks, seven more people in the Lebowa region were burned at the stake and two were hanged. All had been accused of witchcraft, specifically with bringing down lightning, and 18 village elders were under arrest for the murders. At this time of the year, the area is regularly swept by thunderstorms, and people ask their village elders, called *inyangas*, to "sniff out" those who have directed lightning bolts at people and property. By mid-February, 12 alleged witches had been sacrificed, including a man and two women set alight while tied to a truck in Zebediela. Some of the named culprits ran away; others decided to stay and take the punishment, knowing that if they didn't sacrifice themselves, another member of their family would be killed as a substitute.

A UGANDAN RAINMAKER named Kazaalwa threatened, in November 1987, to loose his powers on the village of Rewnyangi unless people showed him more respect and more importantly, perhaps, a little more generosity. A few days later, hailstorms and high winds lashed the village, ripping the roofs off houses, shops and three schools. Angry villagers immediately held the rainmaker responsible, pushing him out into the hailstorm and beating him to death.

•◆•

WICKED INDEED WERE THE EXPLOITS of Datu Mangayanon, the high priest of the Ata tribe, who occupied the remote mountaintop village of Gunitan, Mindanao, one of the Philippine islands. He had promised the villagers that the dried leaves of a tree that he had ritually killed by hacking it would turn into money. The tribe waited for days, in September 1985, but the miraculous money failed to appear. Mangayanon sulked, and the villagers muttered. Finally, the magician offered to put things right by inviting the villagers to a feast where they could eat porridge that would "free them from all hardships." Whoever ate some, he said, "would see the image of God." Naively, everyone except Mangayanon's wife took his words at face value. The porridge was laced with insecticide, and 68 men, women and children died. There were seven survivors, but they were unable to say whether Mangayanon was among the dead. His wife was among them, however; when she refused the porridge, the magician hacked her to death.

•◆•

ROBERT WILLIAMS, 45, claimed to be a witchcraft practitioner, but it didn't seem to do him any good. Having announced his vocation, he lost his job as chief psychologist at the state industrial prison in Hutchinson, Kansas, in 1974. Rather than using magic to get his job back, he shot himself.

Traditional healer Lovemore Mpofu, 40, told his followers in Zimbabwe that his magical powers would allow him to breathe underwater for 48 hours. In September 1990, he organized a tribal cleansing ceremony with a group of trainees at a dam in the southwestern part of the country, and when he plunged into the water and did not surface they believed it was part of the rite. For two days the followers danced and sang on the shore, awaiting his return—but by then he had drowned.

IN CHINA, ZHANG ZHIKE, 25, wanted to become the new emperor. Described as a deeply superstitious peasant, he consulted a local sorcerer in the eastern province of Anhui who told him that his chances were being blocked by a "fox spirit." In Chinese tradition, foxes are believed to be able to magically transform themselves into beautiful, sexually vampiric women, and the sorcerer named the spirit as Zhang's new bride, Lu Zhihua. In fact, the only strange thing about Lu was that she was a Christian who, worried by her husband's strange behavior, had summoned people to read the Bible and pray for him. Perhaps they didn't pray hard enough, for in August 1992, Zhang lured his wife to a deserted spot and killed her. His chances of becoming emperor were rather blighted after his arrest.

# THE ULTIMATE SACRIFICE

———◆———

*Life is the greatest sacrifice we can make—so great, in fact, that people usually sacrifice someone else's instead of their own. We tend to regard human sacrifice as a practice from the distant past, an act of barbarism no modern person could contemplate. And yet, throughout the world, it still goes on for all sorts of reasons: magical, religious, and downright bizarre.*

———◆———

FRANÇOIS GODEFRAY OF BIGONVILLE, Luxembourg, was convinced that beings from outer space would be landing soon. The self-styled prophet was well known to his neighbors as an eccentric, so it didn't seem all that remarkable to them when he began building wooden crates in his garden. But when Rosemarie, the 16-year-old daughter of the woman living with him, disappeared in September 1984, suspicions were heightened. It turned out that Godefray had locked Rosemarie in one of the crates and starved her to death as a virgin sacrifice to alien visitors. "She was pure and untouched by earthly sin," he told police. "I wanted to sacrifice her to the men from another planet who will land soon in a spaceship." The bearded prophet was taken to a mental hospital. No spaceships were reported to have landed.

OUR NEXT TALE is more traditional. The biblical story of Abraham offering his son Isaac as a sacrifice to God is as well known to Muslims as it is to Jews and Christians. In November 1990, a horrible repeat performance occurred, although this time God failed to send an angel to stop the sacrifice. Ibrahim (Abraham) Halil Altun named his instructor as the leader of the Turkish Sunni Muslim Nakshibenbi sect. "My sheikh told me that if one loves his child too much he'll have no love left for God, so I must kill my son," he said. "I took my baby boy Abdullah to a cave and cut him to pieces with a knife. My sheikh said he would bring the child back if I went to a hilltop and shouted Abdullah's name three times. I did so. I did whatever he asked me to do. But my son never came back."

In March 1984, a 16-year-old boy was beheaded by a Chinese medium in Kuala Lumpur, Malaysia, as a sacrifice for a lucky lottery number. No one won the prize that week.

AN UNNAMED FARMER from Sichuan province, in western China, had a dream in March 1991 in which he saw his 78-year-old mother standing in front of their home, holding a golden lotus. He thought the dream was directing him to sacrifice her in order to obtain good fortune, so he buried her alive.

• ◆ •

ONE PERSON MURDERING a parent is bad enough, but when the entire family joins in, that seems to be taking things a bit far. Eight members of an Appalachian Mountain family from Inez, Kentucky, were arrested in February 1933 after Lucinda Mills, 72, was sacrificed by her own relatives. Acting on "divine commands," Mills's sons, daughters, their spouses and her grandson conducted a rite lasting several hours, which included fasting and speaking in tongues, before her son John strangled her with a chain. The body was placed on a crude altar, but police broke down the barred door of the cabin before the rite could continue. The family was taken to jail where, apparently lacking remorse, they shouted, prayed, chanted and danced in their cells.

•◆•

IN CANTAGALO, BRAZIL, in 1979, police arrested two men, Waldir de Souza and Maria de Conceicao Pontes. They were charged with murdering a two-year-old boy, Antonio Carlos Magalhaes, in a voodoo rite; his blood was then used by the men and their employer in another rite to magically secure success for a new cement business. In custody, they confessed to five other human sacrifices, but by then a crowd, 2,000 strong, had gathered outside the police station. Before the two men could show police where the victims were buried, they were sacrificed themselves by the mob, which set fire to police cars, overpowered the guards, beat up the culprits and tossed them into the burning cars.

•◆•

A DROUGHT LASTED FOR many months in Rhodesia in 1922, and the resulting poor crops threatened famine. The elders of the Mtawara tribe held a council, consulted a rain-maker and decided on a tried and trusted remedy: the public burning of a human victim while the people prayed. They carried out their plan, and 63 people were later charged with murder. The drought broke immediately after the sacrifice.

•◆•

THE VILLAGE OF SIPCHE, near Katmandu in northern Nepal, lost all its men in 1972. The women believed that if they sacrificed a hundred men, the hundredth would turn into gold and make them rich, while at the same time the rite would help them get to heaven. So they lured all the men in the village to a feast where they served dishes mixed with harital, a poisonous root. All of them died, but no gold appeared: the village was left inhabited entirely by widows and children.

• ◆ •

AN EIGHT-YEAR-OLD GIRL was kidnapped and sacrificed to the gods in September 1991 by villagers near Delhi, India, in a ritual that involved surrounding her body with cloves and chilies. It was designed to cure another girl of epilepsy. The second girl was believed to be possessed by demons.

• ◆ •

OUR CATALOG OF HORRORS ends on a more pathetic note. Lolita Arellano, 34, from Bacolod on Negros island in the Philippines, was in grief when the eruption of Mount Pinatubo on Luzon Island killed 700 people. So at 3 a.m. one night in November 1991, she took a scythe and beheaded her three sleeping sons, Manny, 7, Everlito, 6, and Romulo, 4. She also slit her wrists, but her sister rushed her to a hospital and she survived. Arellano said she was offering her children's heads to pacify the volcano.

# DEATH BY DOUGHNUT

*Though we must eat to survive, and many of us live to eat, food can also be the death of us.*

SOUTH AFRICAN VICTOR VILLENTI, 50, was a strict vegetarian, and forced his family to follow the same regime. Unlikely as the tale may sound, we're told that while out jogging in 1991, he was killed by an eight-pound frozen leg of lamb that fell from a third-story window and landed on his head.

IN FEBRUARY 1987, Donald Morris Smith, 22, used a giant candy cane to beat the owner of a candy store unconscious in Rocky Mount, North Carolina, after which Smith strangled him. The murderer was sentenced to 70 years.

FRANZ WETTSTEIN WAS only 20 when he died in September 1977, but he weighed 686 pounds and was Europe's fattest man. Franz started his working life as a butcher's errand boy, but was fired when his bicycle collapsed under him. Weighing a mere 420 pounds at the time, his next move was into show business. Billed as the "Eating Machine," he made a meager living as a sideshow attraction, with customers paying 75 cents a head to watch him eat. Festival organizers decided he should fatten up a bit, so his daily intake rose to 35 pints of beer, 30 or 40 bread rolls and five pounds of sausages or ten steaks. Under the terms of his contract, he had to keep on eating until the last customer went home. Eventually he collapsed with heart trouble, but the first ambulance sent to fetch him had to be sent back because it was too small. He survived that attack, but went back to the peep show afterward and continued munching as before, until finally his heart gave out. Relatives accused his managers of abuse.

•◆•

SNAILS WERE MARC QUINQUANDON'S particular fancy. The 27-year-old French train conductor already held the world record for shelling and eating 144 snails in 11 minutes 30 seconds, and was in training for an attempt on 200 when he was guest of honor at a snail dinner in a village near Nancy in November 1979. There he downed 72 snails in three minutes. The next day he collapsed and was rushed to a hospital, but died of indigestion shortly afterward. He weighed 364 pounds when he died. His last words were, "I'm not in shape."

Slapstick comedian Yves Abouchar, 45, choked to death on a custard pie thrown in his face. The French star inhaled just as the pie landed and was suffocated by the meringue.

IN CENTRAL RUSSIA and the Ukraine, a large number of people died in 1992 after eating what should have been perfectly edible mushrooms, such as boletus, russula, saffron, milk cap or chanterelle. It was thought that the mushrooms had drawn an unidentified toxin from the soil or mutated, perhaps because of pollution. The poison attacked the liver and kidneys, in extreme cases causing death within three days. The first 193 cases, including 23 deaths, were reported from an area near a nuclear power plant in the Voronezh region, while in the Ukraine alone 600 took ill. Before the outbreak ended, more than 60 people died.

• ◆ •

IN THE UKRAINE, three 18-year-olds doing national service were sent to clean a 12-foot-deep underground food container in Charkov. They were fatally overcome by pickled-cabbage fumes, as was a 48-year-old worker who went to their rescue.

• ◆ •

ROBERT PUELO, 32, entered a 7-Eleven store in St. Louis on October 10, 1994, and started shouting and cursing. When an employee threatened to call the police, Puelo grabbed a hot dog, stuffed it down his throat and left the store without paying. The police discovered him unconscious and turning purple outside the store. He choked to death before he could be saved.

• ◆ •

IN BANGKOK, THAILAND, a construction worker ate four bags of deep-fried locusts in October 1985. Unfortunately, he didn't take into account how the locusts might have been killed, and he died shortly after, from insecticide poisoning.

• ◆ •

PARISIAN POLICE INVESTIGATING the 1976 death of beautiful Michele Federici could see that she had obviously been murdered: there were six stab wounds in her throat and chest. The most baffling aspect of the case was that the wounds contained traces of Parmesan cheese. Eventually, detective Henri Vantin went to see her husband, Othello, at his grocery shop and asked him if he stocked Parmesan, at which point the shopkeeper broke down in tears and confessed. His wife, 20 years his junior, had spurned his love for months and eventually admitted to an affair with his best friend. Enraged, the aptly named Othello grabbed a jagged piece of hard Parmesan and stabbed her to death with it. He was found guilty of murder, but released after spending two years in jail.

Chef Juan Ruiz was stabbed through the heart with uncooked spaghetti strands when 150-mph winds hit his restaurant in Mexico City.

A DOUGHNUT WAS the murder weapon used in May 1986 by nursing home owner Carol Detlaff, 58, of St. Joseph, Michigan. She became upset when Gladys Mulhern, 59, was playing with her food after the other residents had finished, and stuffed the doughnut into Mulhern's mouth, causing her to choke to death.

• ◆ •

A FLYING TURNIP FLUNG from a passing car fatally injured 56-year-old Leslie Merry as he was walking near his home in Leytonstone, east London, in July 1989. He was believed to be the victim of a vegetable-throwing gang already responsible for 23 incidents of melons, potatoes and cabbages hurled at innocent passersby. Among the most seriously hurt was a jogger who underwent surgery for internal injuries caused by a flying cabbage to the stomach, and a woman who needed treatment for cuts to her face and eye after her glasses were smashed by a potato. Merry was struck from behind and at first thought he had been kicked, but he then saw the turnip rolling away. He was taken to the hospital and treated for a fractured rib, but he died a few days later from a ruptured spleen. Police failed to find the murder weapon but, explaining how anything might be considered an offensive weapon if a person intends to use it in an assault, said, "If a group of youths are walking or driving around at night with raw turnips or similar vegetables, then they are probably not planning to eat them."

•◆•

THREE FIJIAN FISHERMEN choked to death on live fish. All three tried to kill their catch by biting its head. A fisherman from the island of Rabi was the first fatality in December 1994. On January 14, 1995, a fish head lodged in the throat of Samueal Taoba, 50, from a village on the island of Vanua Levu. Its spines were stuck in his esophagus, and he suffocated before friends could pull it out. Serupepeli Lumelume, 22, died the same way on February 14, 1995, while fishing in a river near Narvosa on the island of Viti Levu.

> Abner Kriller, of Albany, Australia, was blowing a chewing gum bubble while driving when it burst and stuck to his glasses. Blinded, he drove off the road and plunged down a hill to his death.

THOUGH NOT A CASE of death by food, death and food are in close proximity in this tale. In October 1992, California health inspectors carried out a routine examination of a fast-food diner in Los Angeles and found two human corpses in the freezer. They were owner Lydia Katash and her lover, who had been strangled at least eight months previously. Police arrested Katash's ex-husband and partner in the business, but the health inspectors were unable to close down the restaurant. If they had found rats or cockroaches, closure would have been instant, but there was no regulation about human bodies stored next to food.

•◆•

A 23-YEAR-OLD candy-factory worker suffocated in marsh-mallows in Marseille, France, in July 1993. A bin filled with 5,000 pounds of soft, sweet stickiness tipped over, and he drowned in the ensuing avalanche.

•◆•

DEATH WAS SWEET, too, for Joseph LaRose, 31, of Tampa, Florida. He was delivering ice cream to a supermarket in April 1991 when a 500-pound rack of Nutter Butters fell on him, breaking his leg and crushing his skull.

# TOOTH & CLAW

---

*We may eat what we like, but is mankind the ruler of the planet? The following stories make clear that we are not always at the top of the food chain.*

---

IN JUNE 1979, a South Korean fisherman was preparing his catch after it had been landed in New Zealand. He thought the tuna he was about to gut was dead, but it flicked its tail, driving the knife he was holding into the luckless man's chest and killing him.

•◆•

SPANISH ANGLER MARIA CISTA, 56, was trying to free the hook from a fish's mouth in July 1983 when the fish jumped out of her hand and into her mouth. She choked to death as it wriggled into her throat.

•◆•

IN SEPTEMBER 1981, an overloaded ferry arrived at Obidos, Brazil, and the 500 passengers crowded to the shore side as it drew up to the dock. The boat capsized, depositing all aboard into a stretch of the Amazon River that happened to be a breeding ground for piranhas. As the screaming passengers struggled to reach the shore, shoals of piranhas ripped into them, attacking again and again in a feeding frenzy that left more than 300 dead.

FOUR BROTHERS between 8 and 15 years old in the western Algerian city of Maghnia died shortly after eating soup in May 1992. Their mother had inadvertently brought home a poisonous snake, hidden among vegetables that she had put in the family refrigerator. When she took them out, the snake, seeking warmth, slithered into the soup pot and discharged its venom.

• ◆ •

IN JUNE 1981, young Ghulam Nabi was mending his motor scooter on the road from Srinagar, India, to his home 15 miles away. As he crouched there, a hawk flew overhead with a live viper in its claws, which it dropped. The snake landed on Nabi's neck and bit him; he died a few minutes later. The hawk, however, retrieved the snake and flew off with it.

Fisherman Anthony Fernando, 21, died in March 1988 off the coast of Sri Lanka when a garfish, which looks much like a swordfish, leaped from the water and speared his neck.

IN BINGEN, GERMANY, Eric Dankert faced a murder charge in January 1982 when his wife, Maria, 31, was shot dead with a rifle as she played the piano. But Dankert, 64, explained that Maria had asked him to show her how the gun worked because she was nervous when left alone in the house. As he held the gun, his Alsatian, Dixie, jumped up at him and pulled the trigger with his paw, shooting Maria dead. When Dixie and the gun were taken into a field and it was shown that the dog could set off the gun, Dankert was freed. Dixie, on the other hand, died soon afterward when he accidentally ate rat poison.

Renate Pancea died of carbon monox-
ide fumes that escaped after mice closed
the chimney of his house in Mantua,
Italy. Three of his relatives were also
fatally gassed as they waited for a priest
to read the last rites.

NEAR TEHERAN IN APRIL 1990, a 27-year-old Iranian
hunter named Ali-Ashgar Ahani tried to catch a live snake
by pressing the butt of his shotgun behind its head. The
snake coiled around the butt and pulled the trigger with its
thrashing tail, firing one of the barrels and shooting Ahani
fatally in the head. As his colleague tried to grab the shotgun, the writhing reptile triggered the other barrel, but the
second shot missed.

•◆•

GIORGIO SCRIMMIN, 55, of Venice, was kept awake by a
howling cat in October 1992. He leaned out of his bedroom
window and tried to hit it with a broom. The terrified
cat leaped over his head onto the roof, where it dislodged
a slab of marble that fell onto Scrimmin's head and
killed him.

•◆•

EVEN SMALL, FURRY ANIMALS can prove less cuddly than
we think. In January 1993, workman Seagan Dawe, 61,
was on a ladder repairing a roof in Quinton, Birmingham,
England, when he cried "Get off! Get off!" before falling
15 feet, landing headfirst on the concrete driveway below.
His skull was fractured, and he died five hours later. He was
bitten by one of a family of squirrels who lived in the roof.

Nanette Meech, 76, of Santa Fe, California, was canoeing down the Brule River in Wisconsin with her daughter, Laurie, on July 15, 1993. On the bank stood a 40-foot poplar tree, about 18 inches in diameter, which had been gnawed by a beaver. As they floated by, the tree crashed down on Laurie's head and killed her.

IN NOVEMBER 1984, a herd of 36 wild elephants destroyed large areas of rice and banana crops in Syamtalira Bayu, Sumatra. Led by a large white bull elephant, they damaged 14 villages. A villager called Hussein tried to defend his crops by grabbing hold of the trunk of the charging white bull and slashing it with a knife. The elephant hurled Hussein ten feet into the air and, when he landed, the herd trampled him to death.

•◆•

IN FEBRUARY 1993, 50-year-old Heibrecht Beukes from Pretoria was walking her dog in the Mabelingwe nature reserve in Transvaal, South Africa. Upset by the dog's barking, an enraged hippopotamus smashed its way through an electrified fence, apparently oblivious to the shocks, and trampled and crushed Beukes to death between its powerful jaws. The hippo was later shot.

# OUT WITH A BANG

---◆---

*Guns, of course, are dangerous weapons,
as are many other things in the hands of
the less than competent. Whether lousy
aim, misidentification or downright stupidity
is to blame, the results are all too often
the same.*

---◆---

TALES OF HUNTERS MISTAKING their colleagues for prey are so common that one wonders whether animal impressionists are becoming an endangered species. For instance, in November 1990, Charles Boyer, 43, went turkey hunting in Deerfield Township, Pennsylvania. In order to get near the birds, he daubed his clothes with blue and gray patches that looked like turkey heads, crouched behind a bush and made gobbling sounds. Ninety yards away, Troy Moore heard him, spotted something moving, and shot Boyer dead.

•◆•

IN YUGOSLAVIA, Dragutin Ilic went off to the woods in October 1978 to practice his rutting stag imitation. He was so good at it that he was shot and killed by a poacher.

•◆•

A NEW ZEALAND FARMER was hunting rabbits with his 10-year-old son in November 1988. They were trying to flush out rabbits from their farmhouse when the boy fell through a trapdoor in the floor and began crawling about between the house piles. Noticing the movement, the farmer fired his rifle, hitting his son in the forehead and killing him.

• ◆ •

A MOTORIST IN NORTHERN NAMIBIA in August 1989 ran over a porcupine, stopped the car, and decided to put the injured animal out of its misery by clubbing it to death with his shotgun. In doing so, he managed to shoot himself dead. What happened to the porcupine was never established.

• ◆ •

IN NOVEMBER 1991, Clarence Lewis, 49, was at home baby-sitting his grandchildren in LaPlace, Louisiana. He got so fed up with watching kids' programs on the television that he pulled out a .45-caliber pistol from under the cushion of his chair and decided he was going to shoot out the screen. His aim being less than perfect, he missed the TV set entirely and shot his wife, Sara, straight through the head.

In November 1993, a teacher at a school in Thailand used a real pistol to start races at the school sports day. As he waved youngsters back after a false start, the gun went off and killed a six-year-old boy.

IN WILMINGTON, CALIFORNIA, an unnamed teenager boasted to his friends about his .38-caliber revolver, in March 1992. Showing off, he fired four or five bullets into the air. One of them hurtled down out of the sky, half a mile away, and hit five-year-old Adrian Benitez in the head as he was walking with his mother and brother. Adrian died six days later when he was taken off a life-support machine. The teenager was tracked down and arrested.

•◆•

AT AN AUSTIN, TEXAS, APARTMENT COMPLEX William Howard Tate, 43, picked up his .45-caliber semiautomatic in June 1988, without realizing that it was loaded. Fortunately for him, he was pointing it at the floor when it went off. Less fortunate was the unnamed man lying in bed in the apartment below Tate's: the bullet went straight through the floor and hit him in the chest. He was pronounced dead at the scene.

•◆•

ROMOLO RIBOLLA, 42, sat in the kitchen of his home near Pisa, Italy, gun in hand and threatening to kill himself. He was depressed because he couldn't find a job. For nearly an hour his wife, Emilia, pleaded with him not to do the deed. Finally, he burst into tears and threw the gun to the floor. It went off and killed her.

•◆•

IN DECEMBER 1987, a 16-year-old student named Lovell was working on a computer at the home of his friend David Duquette, 19, in Glocester, Rhode Island. He began to hiccup, at which point Duquette decided that the best way to cure him was to give him a fright. He went to his parents' room and got a .38-caliber revolver, which he assumed was unloaded. Placing the gun at the back of Lovell's head, he shouted "Bang!" and pulled the trigger. The gun was loaded, and it cured Lovell of his hiccups once and for all.

•◆•

IN OCTOBER 1991, village policeman Marc Fagny, 48, from Arlon in Belgium, was sent to shoot a rabid Alsatian, and ended up killing the woman who owned the dog. At his trial for manslaughter, he said that everybody in the village knew that he couldn't shoot straight.

Two wedding guests died in a gun battle in Aswan, Egypt, after the bride offended family honor by holding her husband's hand, breaking an ancient custom of not showing affection in public.

A TURK IN COPENHAGEN, DENMARK, celebrating a Christmas Eve wedding by firing his gun into the air, killed two guests and wounded nine. The 36-year-old man, whose 12 shots bounced off a concrete ceiling, was charged with manslaughter.

# MURDER
# MYSTERIES

———•◆•———

*We've saved some of the most peculiar
and inexplicable stories for this chapter—
those tales that seem pulled from a
mystery writer's casebook.*

———•◆•———

IN MARCH 1981, heating engineer Roy Orsini of North
Little Rock, Arkansas, was planning to leave home at 4:30
in the morning, to drive to a distant business appointment.
So Orsini, 38, went to bed at 9:00 p.m., and his 33-year-
old wife, Lee, slept with their 13-year-old daughter,
Tiffany, as she usually did when Roy was to get up early,
so she wouldn't be disturbed. Next morning, after breakfast, Lee walked Tiffany to school and then returned home
and began doing the housework. Finishing the downstairs
rooms, she went upstairs and found the bedroom door
locked from the inside. Orsini had never locked the bedroom door before, and when there was no response to her
calls, Lee checked the garage, and she found her husband's
car. Worried, Lee went for help to her neighbor, Glenda
Walker, who brought a hammer and screwdriver, which
they used to break open the door.

Orsini, still in his pajamas, lay facedown on the bed
with a .38-caliber bullet in his head. Suicide was ruled out,
because although Orsini owned a .38, it was in a chest of
drawers several feet from the bed. Obviously, one does not
shoot oneself in the head, put the gun away and return to

lie down on the bed. Tests showed that Orsini had not handled a gun before his death, and his gun was a Smith & Wesson, while the bullet that killed him had come from a Colt. It was undoubtedly murder, apparently carried out between midnight and 1:00 a.m. Yet no one had heard a shot, suggesting that the murder was carried out with a silencer and was probably premeditated. Police could find no motive—or past enemies. There were no fingerprints apart from those of the family, nothing was missing and there were no signs of forced entry. More curious still, the windows were locked from the inside, as was the door, so there seems no way the murderer could have escaped.

•◆•

ANOTHER LOCKED ROOM murder case comes from northern France in August 1966. Bachelor Anton Przewozny, 59, was found beaten to death in his room on a farm at d'Avrainville, Essonne. Other workers heard his cries for help and banged on the locked door of his room. When his cries stopped, they called the police. They found the shotgun that had been used as a bludgeon, in its proper place, but the door had been locked from the inside and the window was bolted. There was soft soil below the 17-foot-high window, but no footprints. And inside the room was another odd clue: there was an ashtray full of cigarette butts. Przewozny did not smoke.

•◆•

IN MAY 1966, Emile Hervé, 47, took ill at his home in the Rue Camille Flammarion in Marseilles. Police inspector Jean Darian drove Dr. Joseph Cambassedes to the house, but when they arrived, a power failure plunged the place into darkness. They were taken upstairs to the sickbed by a member of the family, who lit the way with candles, and they left the door open for light as the doctor examined his patient. They were too late; Hervé had just died. Then the door slammed shut, blowing out the candles, and a gunshot rang out. Almost immediately, the door was opened as the family rushed in to find out what had happened, their candles revealing an astonishing scene. The doctor was face-down over his dead patient, also dead, with blood oozing from a gunshot wound in his back, and on the floor by the inspector was a .22-caliber rifle. Detectives were called, as well as an examining magistrate who ordered an immediate reconstruction of the scene. The dead men were left on the bed, the same candles lit, the door was opened and the rifle, which had already been fingerprinted, was placed back against the wall in its original position. The windows were found to be closed from the inside, there was no sign of an intruder, and all the circumstantial evidence pointed toward Inspector Darian. They went through the reconstruction several times, with the inspector still protesting his innocence, yet it was only near dawn that he was cleared—as he had been implicated—by an accident. A gust of wind blew the door shut, blowing out the candles and knocking down the rifle, which was found with its muzzle pointing toward the bed.

•◆•

NO MURDER MYSTERY is complete without its element of judicial puzzlement. Everyone in the little Syrian village of Kamsihly knew about Abbas Ahmand and his wife, Zehra. The couple had regular noisy quarrels, and Zehra would sometimes turn up at the marketplace with bruises or a black eye. When Abbas himself went to market one day, no one was surprised at his explanation: he told them that Zehra had decided she couldn't live with him anymore, and had left him and the children. The next morning, however, a farmer found the decapitated body of a woman in his cornfield. Some of the villagers identified the body as Zehra's and, with the pair's past record of domestic quarrels, the police arrested Abbas. His protests were not believed, and he was sentenced to life imprisonment. Five years later, in August 1980, Zehra returned to Kamsihly, now 30 years old and unaware that she was officially dead. She explained that she really had left and had got a job in the city, but she missed her children and wanted to see them and Abbas. She was reunited with her kids, who had been raised by relatives, and Abbas was pardoned and released. He went straight home and strangled his wife in front of the children. He told police, "I don't believe that she didn't know I was in jail. She had to pay for my five lost years." Abbas was promptly returned to jail, leaving Syrian lawyers to ponder whether a man can be tried twice for the same murder, even though he was convicted before he committed it.

An unidentified man was found dead on Dartmoor in England, in March 1975, but forensic tests failed to show a cause of death, so police were unable to say whether he met his end as a result of murder, suicide or natural causes. He was wearing a normal suit and shoes that were unsuitable for the moor, carried a detailed ordnance survey map of the area, and had a small amount of cash, but nothing that would identify him. Also in his pockets were 12 hard-to-obtain cyanide capsules containing enough poison to kill 30 people and a bottle of poisonous laburnum seeds, yet there was no trace of either poison in his body. Perhaps most baffling was the remaining item he carried: a bottle of sweet-and-sour sauce.

MORE PUZZLING STILL is the following tale, with its strange and supernatural overtones. Chef Gerald Marten was 26 when he was found dead in his car in the garage of his mother's home in Braintree, England, in August 1981. His mother was on vacation and he had been dead for eight days when he was discovered. It seemed an open-and-shut case, but police stopped the funeral just as the cortege arrived at the crematorium, demanding that the body be taken away for identification tests. It turned out that Marten was indeed the dead man, but an unnamed yet "respectable and responsible" couple who had known him for three years had approached the police and claimed to have met Marten in Braintree's Market Square after he was dead. Police said, "They cannot be dissuaded from the fact that they saw, spoke to and even shook hands with the person they knew as Gerald Marten, two hours after he was found dead and more than a week after he is believed to have died." There seemed to be no rational explanation, but the spokesman continued, "We do not doubt that the couple is telling the truth."

•◆•

JILTED LOVER EDWARD HAND, trying to commit suicide, fired a bullet into his chin. The slug ricocheted off his teeth, out of his right cheek and into the head of his rival, 34-year-old Ronald Gauley, killing him. It took investigators almost four months to figure out what had happened, but they finally arrested Hand, 33, and charged him with third-degree murder. The shooting was the result of a triangle involving Hand, Gauley and Gauley's wife, Kathy. Gauley and his wife had separated in 1993 and Kathy Gauley had moved in with Hand. In June 1994, she moved out and talked of reuniting with her husband. At a tavern called The Twilight Zone, the three met to talk things over on September 23. They all wound up at Hand's trailer in Bartow, 30 miles east of Tampa, Florida, where the incident occurred.

# FUNERAL
# FOLLIES

———•◆•———
*We conclude our stories of death, aptly,
with tales from the funeral parlor and
cemetery. Here we find, all too often, that
the end of life for one is also the beginning
of death for others.*
———•◆•———

AT THANJAVUR, in the southern Indian province of Tamil
Nadu, a Hindu priest was officiating at a funeral in January
1991. In Hindu belief, Yama, the god of death, rides on a
water buffalo with big curling horns whenever he rises up
from hell to pluck away a dying person's soul. It was there-
fore more than slightly appropriate when the priest was
suddenly set upon and gored to death by a water buffalo
maddened by the bite of a rabid dog. The buffalo was later
captured and killed by veterinarians, but by then the god of
death had doubled his tally for the day.

•◆•

AT THE OTHER END of the country, in Srinagar, Kashmir,
90 people were killed at a Muslim funeral in May 1992.
Virtually all of the dead were women, who, according to
custom, do not sit with men on public occasions. Two
hundred women were gathered on the top floor of the
house of Mirza Ghulam Mohammad, whose daughter
Naseema had died of a brain hemorrhage, when the
wooden floorboards collapsed under their weight. They fell

onto 100 more women on the floor below, and then bodies and wreckage crashed through to the ground floor, where a few men were sitting. Apart from the 81 killed on the spot, including Naseema's mother, 100 were injured. Later, in the hospital, some of the injured died from suffocation in the mobs that crammed the wards.

A September 1985 dispute broke out between two brothers-in-law in Vallefiorita, Italy, concerning who was entitled to the last free space in the family tomb. Things soon became so heated that one man stabbed the other to death, thus losing the vacancy to his victim.

A MORE GRISLY TALE comes from Gaenheim, in southern Germany. A 91-year-old woman was certified dead from heart failure and buried in January 1986. After the mourners left, gravedigger Emil Graf was shoveling the earth back into the plot when he heard a knocking, as if the old woman were kicking the coffin lid. He fetched five people from the funeral firm responsible for the ceremony, and for ten minutes they stood around listening as the sounds grew fainter and stopped. Then they carried on and filled in the grave.

•◆•

WE NOW COME TO A TALE that has passed into legend, oft-repeated in various forms. Who knows if or when the events really happened, but the earliest version in our files dates from February 1980. In Bujumbura, Burundi, a man bought a coffin in which to bury a relative and loaded it onto his pickup truck with the help of a friend. Somewhere along the road, the friend slipped into the coffin for a nap and, as the rain started to pour down, closed its lid. Without him knowing it, the driver picked up five hitchhikers, who took their places on the back of the truck; and they, in turn, thought they were riding with an empty coffin. Eventually the friend woke and opened the coffin's lid, causing all five of the hitchhikers to leap off the speeding truck to their deaths.

• ◆ •

IN FEBRUARY 1989, undertaker's assistant Jack Volkering, 59, picked up an encoffined body from a memorial mass and drove it away in his hearse to prepare it for the actual funeral. As he drove along Highway 27 in Cold Spring, Kentucky, a car driven by 23-year-old Lonnie Stephens crossed the road and hit the hearse head-on. Stephens received only minor injuries, but the sudden impact caused the coffin and its contents, weighing 310 pounds, to hurtle forward. It broke through a metal barrier and smashed into Volkering's back, crushing him to death against the steering wheel and dashboard.

In July 1982, the Reverend Ray Hewett had just concluded the burial of Liza Poteete, 91, in Blairsville, Georgia, with the words "we never know who's going next," when a bolt of lightning struck dead her 27-year-old grandson, Donald Metcalf.

IN AUGUST 1992, mourners at a funeral in Larne, England, had to run for their lives to avoid being run over by a limousine with a dead man at the wheel. Hundreds of mourners were walking in the procession around the hearse containing doctor's wife Hilda King, 74, when the two-ton limousine went out of control and plowed into them, leaving three women injured. Slumped at the wheel of the runaway car was funeral director Leslie Adams, 53, who had suffered a heart attack.

FRED DUMELOW, 71, attended the funeral in January 1991 of his lifelong friend Albert Decamps, 75. Unfortunately, after the service began at St. George's church in Ticknell, Derbyshire, England, Dumelow slumped in his pew and died. His body then became wedged between his seat and the one in front, and all efforts to free it failed. After discussions between the Reverend Norman Lifton and the mourners, it was decided to cover Fred's body with a sheet and carry on with the service as normal. As Lifton explained, "The trouble was that we had to be at the crematorium on time. If one funeral is late, all the others are held up. The undertakers were getting agitated." Time and the crematorium schedule, it seems, wait for no man.

In October 1976 a funeral was being held for a fisherman called Ramon at a graveyard in Venezuela. Ramon was not dead but only sleeping, and he woke up in his coffin. He climbed out, cried "I live!" at horrified mourners and then promptly dropped dead from shock. His body was put back in the coffin and the funeral continued.

THE FUNERAL OF BUSINESSMAN William Douch, 52, took place in a tiny Welsh chapel at Brechfa, Dyfed, in December 1989. Douch had died of a heart attack, and all was proceeding normally as Reverend Haydn Richards, 57, took his place in the pulpit and began reading the eulogy. Halfway through, Richards collapsed and, though the mourners rushed to help him, he died, also of a heart attack, before reaching the hospital. Everyone was too upset to carry on, so the funeral was abandoned.

IN MARCH 1980, WHEN the funeral cortege arrived at the cemetery in Gileston, near Cardiff, Wales, they found the grave already occupied. Gravedigger Percy Overton, 54, had just concluded his work when he suddenly collapsed and died, falling into the grave he had just prepared for pensioner Jim Barnes. The service was delayed for 45 minutes while his body was removed.

•◆•

IN SOUTH KOREA, Chun Chong-rok suffered a run of bad luck. A geomancer advised him that this was because his deceased father was still at war with the family, owing to some unspecified grievance, and that the solution was to move his father's tomb. According to Korean tradition, the spirit of the dead will not find proper rest until the body has decomposed, and this seemed to be confirmed when the troublesome father's grave was opened. The body was perfectly preserved after 15 years in the ground. Chun promptly collapsed and died on seeing the corpse; this event presumably brought the dispute to an end.

•◆•

IN JULY 1992, TWO UNDERTAKERS shot each other dead in Paraiba, northeastern Brazil, during an argument over who had the right to conduct the funeral of one of the town's inhabitants. Another undertaker from a neighboring town was called in to bury all three bodies.

# STILL TICKING

Finally we come to those who have avoided all the lethal flying turnips and myriad pitfalls found in earlier chapters to celebrate their centenaries and often far beyond. The Grim Reaper catches up with all of us eventually, but these are the few he seems to have overlooked.

The best scientific advice for living a very long time is to eat less and not get too excited. Gerontological research on animals has shown that the only consistent method of prolonging life is to cut down your calorie count. It doesn't seem to matter how much fat or carbohydrates you eat; you just need the minimum protein, minerals and vitamins required to avoid malnutrition. In societies with a high proportion of centenarians, the people are small and consume about 40 percent fewer calories than we Western fat cats.

There are always exceptions, of course. American junk dealer Richard Lewis survived to the age of 105. He consumed nearly four pounds of sugar a month in his drinks, a dozen eggs a week, a bottle (sometimes two) of Thunderbird wine every day, pounds of streaky bacon dipped in grease, a family-size tub of fried chicken every weekend and ten cigars a day.

Inevitably, centenarians are asked for the key to longevity, and their advice is often startling. Mrs. Bastolumas,

*112, interviewed in her usual deck chair on the beach at Fontabella, Barbados, said the secret was "plenty of sex, plenty of sun, plenty to drink, no work and no children." Louisa Wright, age 107, attributed her health to "always getting my own way." Augusta Holtz, age 117, hit on the irrefutable secret behind a long life: "having birthdays."*

*The stories that follow were gathered by* Fortean Times *editors over the course of the last several years from newspaper reports around the globe. As such, we cannot guarantee that all of these folks are still with us, though no doubt many of them continue to beat the odds. Most of the centenarian claimants over 120 come from parts of the world where proof-of-age documentation is not available; seasoned Forteans, however, know better than to discount such claims with certainty.*

——— •◆• ———

JEANNE MARIE CALMENT, now 121 years old, is the "official" longevity champion. She celebrated her 121st birthday in a retirement home in Arles, in southern France, on February 21, 1996. "I'm afraid of nothing and I don't complain," she said. "I have only one wrinkle, and I'm sitting on it." A week earlier, she had recorded a four-track CD, called "The Mistress of Time," recounting her memories over a musical background of rap, techno and *farandole*, a regional medieval dance tune. "God must have forgotten me," she is fond of saying. She claims the keys to longevity are olive oil and port. Though blind and wheelchair-bound, she is still sprightly with an undimmed memory. She recalls selling colored pencils to Vincent van Gogh and watching the construction of the Eiffel Tower.

André-François Raffay, a lawyer, bought Calment's apartment in Arles in 1965, agreeing under the *viager* system to pay her a fixed sum of 2,500 francs a month until her death, whereupon he would become the owner. However, Raffay died on Christmas Day 1995, aged 77, by which time he had paid out about 900,000 francs, at least three times the value of the apartment. On her birthday every year she sent him a card with the mischievous phrase; "Sorry, I'm still alive." Now, Raffay's widow is obliged to keep sending Calment that monthly check.

•◆•

DJEDALA GOUAS, ALGERIA'S OLDEST WOMAN, died in October of 1988 at the age of 144. She never went to a doctor, but she consulted herbalists. She was survived by a 108-year-old son and a 98-year-old daughter.

•◆•

AMM ATWA MOUSSA, alleged in Egyptian newspaper reports to be over 150, lived with his first wife for 60 years and later married four women, who bore him seven children. He recalls his escape with his family to El Faylum Lake, 62 miles southwest of Cairo, so that the family would not be forced to work on the Suez Canal in 1859. He has worked since then as a fisherman.

Dorah Ramothibe was born in South Africa on June 27, 1881, and attributes her health at 114 to a diet of locusts, pumpkin seeds, tortoise meat, wild herbs, dried fruit and coffee for breakfast. She lives in a Johannesburg retirement home.

ANNIE SCOTT, Britain's oldest person, died on April 21, 1996, at the age of 113. Her husband, Thomas, an auctioneer, died in 1937, and she moved to Scotland in 1971. She is survived by her daughter, Nan, 79, and her son, Tom, 76. A strict Presbyterian who never touched alcohol or tobacco, Scott remained sprightly until the end, although she went blind in the last few months. She never took any medicine, not even an aspirin.

• ◆ •

GONG LAIFA, "CHINA'S METHUSELAH," was supposedly born in March 1848 and died in his hometown in Guizou province on March 12, 1995, of acute jaundice caused by hepatitis at the age of 147. He was four feet, seven inches tall, weighed just over 66 pounds and remained a bachelor all his life. He was recognized as China's oldest person by the China National Committee on Aging on October 22, 1993. They checked his age through family records and by his own memory of historical events. Gong enjoyed a daily tipple of rice wine.

• ◆ •

ZOLFALI SOLTANMORADI, AN IRANIAN, died in February 1995, reportedly 140 years old, leaving 121 descendants in four generations.

• ◆ •

RAIMUNDO GOMES DE SANTOS, 133 years old, was the son of slaves brought from Angola to Brazil by Portuguese traders in the mid-19th century. He worked on a Minas Gerais coffee plantation during his youth, until slavery was abolished in 1888, and he moved to the state of São Paulo, where he eventually bought his own plot of land. He has reportedly never been ill, though he visited the hospital a few years ago after he was hit by a truck.

Henry Govier, of Aversham, England, who was sent home to die in his twenties after being gassed in World War I, celebrated his 102nd birthday in 1992. "My tip for a good, strong heart is neat whisky and dark chocolate."

SALEEM BIN NASEEB AL HADDAD AL HAJRI died at the age of 130 on February 10, 1995, in Wilayat Bidiya, Oman. He was survived by three sons and a large number of grandchildren. He enjoyed good health and his memory was excellent. He lived in a tent next to his house and disdained the use of electricity.

•◆•

CHRISTIAN MORTENSEN WAS BORN on August 17, 1882, and at 113 is the world's oldest man whose age can be verified beyond dispute. He lives in San Francisco.

•◆•

MARIA DO CARMO JERONIMO celebrated her 125th birthday on March 4, 1996, with a Catholic mass and a chocolate cake in her hometown of Itajuba, Brazil, where she moved in 1942. On February 19, she took pride of place on a float in the Rio Carnival, where she played the grandmother of Zumbi, a 17th-century leader of a black slave revolt against the Portuguese who was assassinated in an ambush.

Jeronimo doesn't have official birth records, but a local Catholic church issued a baptismal certificate for her in Carmo de Miñas on March 21, 1871, when she was 17 days old. An African Brazilian who is only four feet, one inch tall, she was a slave until May 1885, when slavery was abolished in Brazil. In 1995 she was still walking two kilometers each day to attend mass, had good eyesight and drank some wine daily. She has only been ill once: at the age of 120, she was taken to the hospital with pneumonia and hypoglycemia, but recovered in ten days. She hates only two things in life: marriage and shoes.

Prom Kaewerorarm of Bangkok was planning in 1993 at the age of 115 to marry his third wife, Bai Ohnok, 106. They had met at a health contest for the elderly. Recipe for longevity: "No smoking, no drinking, plenty of fish and fruit— plus five hot, fried chili peppers every day to keep you regular."

SUSIE BRUNSON WAS BORN IN NEW YORK CITY on Christmas Day 1870, the child of freed slaves, and died in December 1994, 16 days shy of her 124th birthday. She was married three times and had 12 children, all but one of whom died before their tenth birthday. Her age cannot be proved, because the family Bible listing her date of birth was stolen in 1932. A longtime resident of Roosevelt, Long Island, she moved to Wilmington, North Carolina, in 1987, when she was 116. She is survived by her daughter, Mary McDaniel, 84, of Wilmington.

•◆•

ATIDJE STARKOVA, BULGARIA'S oldest woman, died on January 24, 1996, at the age of 120, at her home in the village of Sinya Voda in the northeast of the country. Official documents show that she was born on May 12, 1875, three years before Bulgaria regained its independence from Ottoman rule.

MARGARET SKEETE DIED AT 115 in Radford, Virginia, on May 7, 1994, bedridden since a fall three weeks earlier. Her age is verified by a Texas census of 1880 that listed her as two years old. Her formula for longevity: eat plenty of sweets.

Bushtai Brezenian, 138 years old, found fame in 1991 in the autonomous Caucasian republic of Chechen-Ingush with his lover Giorgi Salmessi, 130. The gay couple fell in love in 1881 and were persuaded to come out of the closet on their 110th anniversary by local activists.

REBECCA HEWISON, born Rebecca Ramsdale, on October 19, 1881, died at the age of 112 on September 22, 1994, in Grimsby, England, where she was born. Married in 1905 to stonemason George Hewison, who died in the 1920s, she was a soccer fanatic and ardent supporter of Grimsby Town. She attributed her longevity to a regular glass of port and lemon.

•◆•

MANOEL DE MOURA, a farm laborer from Cerrito Alegre in Brazil, was still smoking 80 to 100 cigarettes a day in 1984, when he was alleged to be over 160. He said, "I don't own anything and I don't worry about anything." Possessing a birth certificate that indicated he was born on March 25, 1819, he was remembered by elderly fellow villagers as an old man when they were children.

SHIGECHIYO IZUMI GAVE UP SMOKING AT 116, but continued to drink a daily dram of sugar cane liquor until he died at 120 on February 21, 1986. He was four feet, eight inches tall, ate mostly grain and vegetables and advised, "Leave things to God, the Sun, and Buddha."

• ◆ •

IKE WARD, A WOODCUTTER born into slavery on December 25, 1862, died in January 1982 at the age of 119. He was raised near Richmond, Virginia, then moved to Daytona Beach, Florida, where he lived his last 50 years. He married and outlived 16 wives, did his own cooking and washing and plowed his own one-acre plot until two weeks before his death.

• ◆ •

JACKSON POLLARD WAS REPORTEDLY 123 while living in the Long Term Care Unit of Central State Hospital in Milledgeville, Georgia, in January 1990. He claims he was born on Chrismas Day 1866 and fought in both the Spanish American War and World War I. His advice: "Avoid alcohol, eat good vegetables, never, never get married to no skinny woman, smoke a good pipe and trust in God."

• ◆ •

FRANCISCO BARRIOSNUEVO CHOPERANA, Colombia's oldest man, turned 125 on October 2, 1995, in the small northern town of Majagual, 40 years after he made a coffin for himself in case he didn't make 85. Choperana, only four feet seven inches tall, drinks four liters of milk a day and sits constantly in his rocking chair listening to the sound of a nearby river. He walks with a cane and is slightly deaf, but maintains "I do everything on my own." He claims to have fought in a Colombian civil war at the turn of the century. He has 49 grandchildren and ten great-grandchildren, and fathered his last child when he was 90.

# SOURCES

———•◆•———

## CUPID'S DEADLY DARTS

Ferrozzo: *Daily Mail, Daily Mirror,* Nov. 25, 1988.
Daniels: *Times-Reporter* (Ohio), Jan. 22, *Daily Express,* Jan. 23, 1988.
Hidaka: *D. Mirror,* Oct. 11, 1992.
Min: *Celebrity,* Nov. 19, 1987.
Brayboy: *Independent,* Dec. 7, 1990.
Dunja: *News of the World,* June 15, 1980.
Paler: *News on Sunday,* Nov. 8, 1987.
Farrand: *Weekend,* July 19, 1978.
Cantori: *Dracula* (Romania), June 1, 1993.
Momescu: *Weekend,* July 12, 1978.
Kneen: *Daily Telegraph,* Apr. 8, 1993.
Turkish roof falls: *Guardian,* Nov. 16, 1990.
Nelson: *D. Record,* Mar. 22, 1993.
Orionno: *D. Mirror,* Oct. 24, 1988.
Newman: *D. Telegraph,* July 14, 1992.
Ancoretti: *S. Express,* July 1, 1984.

## WEDDING WOES

Weltz: *People,* Sept. 12, 1993.
Mathai: *Sunday Express,* July 10, 1977.
Guy: *Western Morning News,* June 21, 1993.
Cundiff: *D. Mail,* June 26, 1979.
Yang: *Xinmin Evening News,* June 11, 1991.
N. Carolina couple: *Guardian,* June 8, 1987.
Jordanian wedding: *Guardian,* Oct. 1, 1990.

Hoffmann: *D. Record,* Oct. 21, 1991.
Zhang: *E. Standard,* Feb. 18, 1992.
Nasrul: *S. Mail,* September 23, 1990.

## TEMPER TEMPER

Corlett: *D. Telegraph,* July 9, 10, 15, 1987.
Allen: *Pawtuxet Valley Daily Times,* July 12, 1986.
Dominguez: *D. Star,* Nov. 27, 1992.
Love: *S. Mail,* Oct. 20, 1991.
Mancuso: *S. Express,* Nov. 18, 1990.
Taylor: *D. Telegraph,* Mar. 9, 1991.
Casanova: *Weekend,* May 31, 1978.
Jeurgens: *S. Mail,* Sept. 9, 1990.
St. Marcel schoolboy: *Reveille,* Mar. 24, 1978.
Smith: *[Associated Press],* Aug. 22, 1994.
Mori: *Sun,* July 3, 1986.
Lumia: *Sun,* Mar. 25, 1993.
D'Alessio: *News of the World,* Feb. 28, 1993.
Hicks: *The Scotsman,* Dec. 10, 1986.
Sun: *Guardian,* Oct. 17, 1987.
Guy: *D. Telegraph,* July 23, 1988.
Musgrove: *Los Angeles Times,* Aug. 17, 1994.

## LOONY LOSSES

Zumner: *Daily Record* (Scotland), Oct. 21, 1994.
Pitioret: *D. Record,* Mar. 24, 1993.
Kell: *N.Y. Post,* Oct. 27, 1994.

Townsend: *North Devon Journal-Herald,* Apr. 22, 1982.
Brooklyn Bridge man: *D. Mirror,* May 18, 1993.
Chicken/egg argument: *S. Times,* Jan. 15, 1978.
Santos and Ja: *The Orcadian,* June 11, 1987.
Philippines beauty argument: *D. Telegraph,* June 13, 1987.
Mitchell: *Times,* Mar. 29, 1975.
Johnson: *D. Telegraph,* Oct. 28, 1992.
Lecuere: *Celebrity,* June 30, 1988.
Austin man: *[Reuters],* May 11, 1983.
Grundman: *D. Mail,* Aug. 17, 1990.
Pinelli: *Sun,* June 18, 1993.
Hamm: *Victoria Times-Colonist,* Jan. 29, 1989.
Hommel: *People,* Oct. 10, 1993.
Alicante con man: *Johannesburg Citizen,* May 16, 1991.
Dalhanna: *S. Mail,* Mar. 28, 1993.
Barrera: *Europa Times,* Jan. 1994.
Singh: *D. Mirror,* Nov. 20, 1992.
Chinese soldiers: *Guardian,* June 13, 1984.
Jules: *D. Record,* Jan. 2, 1992.
Tollett: *Times, D. Telegraph,* Feb. 13, 1995.

### SNOW JOBS

Bowers: *Shropshire Star,* Jan. 16, *D. Express,* Jan. 17, 1980.
Morrell: *D. Mail, D. Express,* Mar. 1, 1989.
Rutelli: *D. Record,* Feb. 28, 1991.
Gados: *Unidentified U.S. newspaper,* Dec. 30, 1988.
German pilots: *Sun,* Mar. 12, 1984.
Winter: *D. Mirror,* Jan. 10, 1984.
Sanchez: *D. Express,* Oct. 11, *Independent,* Oct. 12, 1990.
Heer: *D. Telegraph,* Jan. 10, 1986.

Smalls: *D. Telegraph,* Jan. 22, 1981.
Reader: *D. Post, D. Telegraph,* Apr. 27, 1990.

### REVENGE OF THE MACHINES

Gooch: *D. Mirror,* Apr. 20, *The Record* (NJ), Apr. 5, 1988.
Gudkov: *Sun,* Mar. 5, 1992.
Niskala: *Victoria Times-Colonist,* Sept. 18, 1987.
Davis: *D. Mirror,* Apr. 22, 1991.
Rodriguez: *Atlanta Journal & Constitution,* Dec. 4, 1988.
Thomas: *Boston Globe,* Aug. 13, 1987.
Bronx factory worker: *Daily Star,* June 25, 1994.
Penna: *Daily Record, Daily Star,* Jan. 9, 1995.
Prado: *N.Y. Daily News,* May 12, 1992.
Maguire: *S. Press,* Jan. 10, 1993.
Castro: *D. Star,* Jan. 9, 1991.
Aierguma: *Independent,* July 30, 1991.
Magnasco: *Sun,* Aug. 23, 1993.

### JUST COINCIDENCE?

Parker: *D. Telegraph,* Jan. 9, 1987.
New Orleans lifeguards: *Sun,* Apr. 16, 1992.
Collier: *Birmingham Evening Mail,* Dec. 8, 1971.
Cave: *D. Post,* June 18, 1982.
Kolominn: *E. Standard,* Apr. 19, 1988.
Stewart: *North West Arkansas Times,* Apr. 7, 1983.
Smoke: *Bay City Times Press,* Aug. 13, 1901.
Ebbin: *Liverpool Echo,* July 21, 1975.
Slabbert: *D. Mirror,* Oct. 13, 1987.
Doucette: *Augusta Chronicle,* Feb. 25, 1990.
Graziano: *S. Express,* Oct. 7, 1984.

Orr: *Manchester Evening News,* Oct. 8, 1991.
Squelch: *D. Telegraph,* Aug. 13, 1987.
Veroni: *La Repubblica* (Italy), Nov. 9, *D. Telegraph,* Nov. 10, 1995.
French avalanche: *D. Mirror,* Dec. 29, 1980.

### DOMINO DEATHS

Montoya: *Nairobi Standard,* Oct. 24, 1988.
Zabolotye: *Guardian,* June 21, 1988.
Menominee: *Dominion* (N.Z.), July 31, 1989.
Nazlat Imara: *[AP],* Aug. 1, *Today,* Aug. 2, *Le Matin* (Berlin), Aug. 4, 1995.
Harrison: *Sun,* Nov. 16, 1990.
Craven family: *D. Telegraph,* Aug. 31, *D. Mirror,* Sept. 1 and 4, 1990.
Limani: *D. Telegraph,* Aug. 17, 1984.
Kinnow: *Weekend,* Aug. 12, 1981.

### TAKE TWO

Zarif: *Independent,* Oct. 7 and 8, 1992.
Philippou: *D. Telegraph,* Jan. 27, 1990.
Millbank: *Independent,* Jan. 23, 1993.
Luise: *S. Express,* Feb. 13, 1983.
Chan: *Independent,* July 12, 1991.
Kreekmore: *S. Express,* Feb. 3, 1985.
Quinanola: *Houston Post,* Sept. 13, 1990.
Schwartz: *S. Express,* Dec. 11, 1983.
Godwin: *Independent,* Mar. 8, 1988.
Knox: *D. Telegraph,* Apr. 1, 1981.
Rio Negro man: *D. Telegraph,* Aug. 12, 1977.

### NATURAL SELECTION

Ito: *Sun,* Sept. 26, 1979.
Polish poacher: *Birmingham Mail,* May 5, 1995.
Sutherland: *San Jose Mercury News,* June 20, 1993.
Iorga: *Sunday Mail* (Scotland), June 12, 1994.
Smith: *News of the World,* Oct. 16, 1993.
Symanski: *Guardian,* Apr. 27, 1993.
Oki: *S. Express,* Aug. 4, 1985.
Butterick: *Vancouver Sun,* Mar. 11, 1980.
Sharland: *D. Telegraph,* Aug. 18, 1989.
Newt man: *Beaumont Enterprise & Journal,* Aug. 11, 1981.
Dorran: *D. Mirror,* July 30, 1992.
Golden: *Boston Globe,* Mar. 14, 1980.
Hallas: *Guardian, D. Telegraph,* Dec. 18, 1979.
Tyree: *Cincinnati Enquirer,* Oct. 2, 1988.
Montpol: *S. Express,* Oct. 6, 1985.
New York man: *New Sunday Times,* July 10, 1977.
Charles: *D. Mirror,* Nov. 12, 1987.
Ramos: *Guardian, D. Telegraph,* Dec. 18, 1979.
Constantino: *S. Express,* June 28, 1987.
Priestley: *D. Telegraph,* Jan. 1, 1979.

### SUICIDE IS PAINFUL

Quinn: *Daily Record,* Aug. 31, 1994.
East London cliff death: *Weekly News,* Dec. 15, 1979.
McCraw: *Europa Times,* Apr. 1994.
Killington: *D. Mirror,* Apr. 24, 1981.
Bennett: *D. Mirror,* Sept. 26, 1991.
Frankenstein: *News-Sun* (Illinois), Mar. 11, 1981.

Auckland electrician: *Middletown Record* (U.S.), Mar. 25, 1973.

Brun: *Victoria Times-Colonist,* Sept. 1, 1987.

Robins: *D. Post,* Sept. 6, 1988.

Chinese peasant girls: *Evening Post* (N.Z.), Oct. 17, 1988.

Chinese pensioners: *South China Morning Post,* May 21, 1993.

Chinese hell tourists: *Belfast Telegraph,* Aug. 5, 1993.

Cazanga: *Aberdeen Press & Journal,* Sept. 1, 1995.

Ruga: *D. Mail,* Oct. 25, 1995.

## JUST FOLLOWING ORDERS

Gonzales: *Houston Chronicle,* Feb. 16, 1981.

Donaldson: *Toronto Sun,* Mar. 31, 1993.

Greco: *Victoria Times-Colonist,* Feb. 25, 1989.

Dowdeswell: *D. Telegraph,* May 19, 1979.

Pickney: *D. Star,* July 15, 1992.

Trofimov: *Cleveland Plain Dealer,* Nov. 3, 1988.

Chinese sons: *D. Telegraph,* Apr. 6, 1985.

Vernicci: *News on Sunday,* Aug. 8, 1987.

## CULT MADNESS

Maneja: *Guardian,* Aug. 12, 1995.

Philippine villagers: *Reveille,* May 11, 1979.

Haigler: *D. Express,* July 5, 1982.

Kumbakonam bathers: *Guardian,* Feb. 19, 1992.

Khadeshwari: *Times of India,* Nov. 5, 1980.

Hapur battle: *Independent,* Feb. 15, 1992.

Azninski: *N.Y. Daily News,* Mar. 14, 1994.

Tanzanian Pathfinders: *San Francisco Chronicle,* Nov. 29, 1993.

Maurice: *Guardian,* Mar. 17, 1976.

Faaite islanders: *The Garden Island* (Hawaii), Mar. 30, 1990.

Sun: *Saudi Gazette,* May 12, 1987.

## BLACK MAGIC

Camus: *S. Express,* Mar. 7, 1976, *Guardian,* May 13, *D. Mail,* May 14, 1977.

Zimbabwe witch doctors: *[AFP],* Dec. 9, 1995.

Delamare: *S. Express,* Apr. 23, 1978.

Lebowa witch burnings: *Guardian,* Jan. 6, Feb. 7, *D. Telegraph,* Feb. 21, 1984, etc.

Kazaalwa: *Victoria Times-Colonist,* Nov. 16, 1987.

Mangayanon: *E. Standard,* Sept. 19, *S. Telegraph,* Sept. 22, 1985.

Williams: *D. Express,* Aug. 6, 1974.

Mpofu: *Houston Post,* Sept. 27, 1990.

Lu Zhihua: *New Straits Times,* Aug. 4, 1992.

## THE ULTIMATE SACRIFICE

Godefray: *D. Mirror,* Sept. 24, 1984.

Altun: *D. Telegraph,* Nov. 28, 1990.

Kuala Lumpur boy: *D. Mirror,* Mar. 21, 1984.

Sichuan farmer: *Independent,* Mar. 24, 1991.

Mills: *Morning Post,* Feb. 10, 1933.

Magalhaes: *The Province,* Oct. 23 and 27, 1979.

Mtawara tribe: *D. News,* Feb. 19, 1923.

Sipche villagers: *D. Express,* (date unknown), 1972.
Delhi girl: *D. Star,* Sept. 26, 1991.
Arellano: *[AP],* Nov. 10, 1991.

## DEATH BY DOUGHNUT

Villenti: *People,* Mar. 27, 1991.
Smith: *Ashbury Park Press,* Feb. 10, 1989.
Wettstein: *S. People,* Sept. 25, 1977.
Quinquandon: *D. Telegraph,* Nov. 27, 1979.
Abouchar: *D. Star,* May 19, 1994.
Ukrainian mushrooms: *D. Telegraph,* Aug. 7, *N.Y. Post,* Aug. 10, 1992.
Ukrainian youths: *[R],* Feb. 25, 1995.
Puelo: *[AP],* Oct. 12, 1994.
Bangkok man: *Guardian,* Oct. 7, 1985.
Federici: *Weekend,* May 3, 1978.
Ruiz: *N.Y. Post,* Oct. 27, 1994.
Mulhern: *N.Y. Post,* Nov. 14, 1988.
Merry: *D. Mirror,* July 27, 1989.
Fijian fishermen: *[R],* Jan. 16, Feb. 17, 1995.
Kriller: *Daily Mail,* Nov. 17, 1994.
Katash: *D. Mirror,* October 27, 1992.
Marseille worker: *D. Record,* July 15, 1993.
LaRose: *Times-Reporter,* Apr. 11, 1991.

## TOOTH & CLAW

South Korean fisherman: *Shropshire Star,* June 4, 1979.
Cista: *Sun,* July 25, 1983.
Obidos ferry: *D. Star,* Sept. 21, 1981.
Maghnia boys: *[AFP],* May 4, 1992.
Nabi: *D. Telegraph,* June 15, 1981.
Fernando: *Sun,* Mar. 9, 1989.
Dankert: *Sun,* Feb. 1, 1982.
Pancea: *Today,* Dec. 28, 1993.
Ahani: *AP Wire,* Apr. 24, 1990.
Scrimmin: *D. Star,* Oct. 5, 1992.
Dawe: *D. Star,* Jan. 28, 1993.

Meech: *Denver Post,* July 17, 1993.
Hussein: *Jakarta Post,* Nov. 24, 1984.
Beukes: *Seychelles Nation,* Feb. 27, 1993.

## OUT WITH A BANG

Boyer: *Sun,* Nov. 2, 1990.
Ilic: *S. People,* Oct. 22, 1978.
New Zealand farmer's son: *D. Telegraph,* Nov. 13, 1988.
Namibian motorist: *Bild Zeitung,* Aug. 10, 1989.
Lewis: *D. Star,* Nov. 4, 1991.
Thai teacher: *D. Mirror,* Nov. 17, 1993.
Benitez: *D. Mirror,* 1992.
Tate: *Laredo Morning Times,* June 10, 1988.
Ribolla: *S. Express,* Apr. 5, 1981.
Lovell: *Baltimore Sun,* Dec. 15, 1987.
Fagny: *D. Record,* Oct. 12, 1991.
Aswan couple: *D. Mail,* Nov. 27, 1995.
Copenhagen Turk: *[R],* Dec. 27, 1995.

## MURDER MYSTERIES

Orsini: *S. Express,* Mar. 29, 1981.
Przewozny: *D. Mirror,* Aug. 18, 1966.
Marseilles mystery: *S. Express,* May 16, 1976.
Ahmand: *S. Express,* Aug. 31, 1980.
Dartmoor man: *S. Express,* July 3, 1977.
Marten: *S. Mirror,* Aug. 23, 1981.
Gauley: *[AP],* Jan. 7, 1995.

## FUNERAL FOLLIES

Thanjavur priest: *N.Y. Post,* Jan. 16, 1991.
Mohammad: *San Jose Mercury News,* May 5, 1992.

Vallefiorita brothers: *Scotsman*, Sept. 5, 1986.
Gaenheim woman: *D. Record*, Jan. 14, 1986.
Bujumbura hitchhikers: *D. Telegraph*, Feb. 13, 1980.
Volkering: *Chillicothe Gazette*, Jan. 14, 1989.
Metcalf: *Guardian*, July 14, 1982.
Adams: *D. Record*, Aug. 28, 1992.
Dumelow: *D. Star*, Jan. 24, 1991.
Ramon: *S. People*, Oct. 17, 1976.
Richards: *Sun*, Dec. 14, 1989.
Overton: *D. Mirror*, Mar. 8, 1990.
Chong-rok: *D. Telegraph*, July 14, 1990.
Paraiba undertakers: *D. Telegraph*, July 28, 1992.

## STILL TICKING

Calment: *[AP]*, Feb. 22, 1991, *Guardian*, Mar. 3, 1993, *[T]*, Feb. 21, *Western Morning News*, Feb. 22, 1994.
Gouas: *Nairobi Nation*, Oct. 4, 1988.
Moussa: *[AP]*, Sept. 4, 1995.
Ramothibe: *Wolverhampton Express & Star*, July 28, *Sunday Express*, July 30, 1995.
Scott: *D. Mail*, Mar. 15, 1995, *Edinburgh Eve. News*, Mar. 15, *Independent, Guardian, Eastern Eve. News*, Apr. 22, 1996.
Gong: *China Daily*, Mar. 1, *Sun*, Mar. 31, 1995.
Soltanmoradi: *[AFP]*, Feb. 13, 1995.
De Santos: *Guardian*, Oct. 14, 1994.
Al Hajri: *Times of Oman*, Feb. 13, 1995.
Mortensen: *Morning Star*, Aug. 15, 1995.
Jeronimo: *Folha de São Paulo*, Mar. 5, *Canberra Times*, Mar. 8, 1995, *South China Morning Post*, Feb. 10, *N.Y. Post, Lewision (ME) Sun-Journal*, Feb. 20, *Glasgow Herald*, Mar. 6, 1996.
Kaewerorarm: *Sunday Telegraph*, Apr. 4, *People*, June 13, 1993.
Brunson: *[AP]*, Dec. 1, 1994.
Starkova: *[R]*, Jan. 25, 1996.
Skeete: *Int. Herald Tribune, D. Post, [T]*, Jan. 5, 1990.
Brezenian: *People* (South Africa), June 9, *Independent*, Dec. 24, 1991.
Hewison: *[T]*, *D. Mail*, Sept. 24, 1994.
De Moura: *Tidbits*, Dec. 1, 1979, *National Enquirer*, July 31, 1980.
Izumi: *S. Times*, Feb. 23, 1986.
Ward: *[AP]*, *Guardian*, Jan. 26, 1982.
Pollard: *Sun Capitol* (Maryland), Jan. 21, 1990, *National Enquirer*, Dec. 12, 1989.
Choperana: *[AP]*, Oct. 3, *Guardian*, Oct. 5, 1995.

# WELCOME TO THE WORLD OF THE BIZARRE AND THE BEWILDERING

From UFOs, Bigfoot and visions of the Virgin Mary to weird tales and human oddities, *Fortean Times* is a respected chronicler of strange phenomena with 24 years' experience of reporting from wild frontiers. Informed, open-minded, skeptical, and above all extremely funny, *FT* has the low-down on what's out there.

Write or call for details of our latest subscription offers. Or send for a sample issue for just $4.95. (You can pay by credit card using our order hotline, or with a check payable to Fenner, Reed & Jackson.)

'The only thing predictable about *Fortean Times* is that it will be unpredictable, which makes it great fun to read."
—*The Boston Globe*

"Immensely entertaining.... A great, roaring sense of humor."
—*Contra Costa Times*

"Bringing wit and erudition to outlandish subject matter."
—*The New York Times*

"Possibly the most entertaining publication on the planet."
—*Wired*